MADRID
in your hand

editorial **en su mano**

First Edition November 1984
© Editorial En Su Mano
c/Ferraz, 34. 28008 Madrid
Tel. 433 82 99
Text by José del Corral
Technical Advisors: Pablo M. Valdés and
José María F. Gaytán
Photographs by M. Corral, Tomás Ruiz and
the State Scretariat of Tourism
and Patrimonio Nacional.
Graphic Design by Florencio García
Map: Ed. ALMAX
Aerial photography by FOTOGRAFIA F3,
S. A.
Type-setting: GRAFILIA, S. L
Process engraving: OCHOA
Binding: PERELLON
ISBN: 84-86.320-06-2
Depósito legal: M-40.108-1984
Printing: EGRAF, S. A.
Polígono Industrial de Vallecas c/G, s/n.
28031 Madrid.
Paper: Granada matte 160 grs./m^2 PAMESA
Printed in Spain
Translated by Muriel Feiner

Where Spring set up Residence

As Spring, like scenery, is nothing more than a state of mind and soul, we can mention Lope de Vega's famous verse:

«Fortunately, it is said by all
that Spring came to Madrid to reside.»

And Calderón de la Barca: «In Madrid, homeland to all / for in its small world / both natives and foreigners / are equally loved children.» Many books have been filled with praise for this Madrid of ours, praise which grows day by day. A few words will suffice to describe this city, its history, its legends and its presence. For above all else is that special, undefinable charm which the city possesses. Madrid is an air and a style, something which we cannot find in photographs but in one way, it is there and for someone who knows Madrid, these illustrations will enrich and complete our own inexpressible memories.

Ask..., and the lover of Madrid will establish his preferences in different ways. There are big streets in Madrid —the Gran Vía, the Calle Alcalá, the Castellana and even the Salón del Prado (imagine calling a place intended for pedestrians and cars a «Salon»); there is a Madrid of overwhelming beauty and stately, cultured and peaceful prominence, which includes the Prado Museum, the Church of Los Jerónimos, the Academy, beside Retiro Park, with its swans which glide along the waters of its fountains; and there is a Madrid of a daring Viaduct, an astonishing Campo del Moro, at the foot of a Palace, which is like a magic crystal formation, beside the Park of the West, which lights up with roses which look with the eyes of Velázquez in the direction of the blue or snow-capped horizon; a Madrid with its Michelangelo Plaza Mayor, or the Teatro Real, and the Plaza de Oriente, with horses of bronze which want to fly; a Madrid of the Manzanares river, the Segovia Bridge and the San Antonio Sanctuaries, and the romantic tear of the Sacramentales; a tall and cosmopolitan Madrid and another which is caught up in the Medieval, the Baroque and the Renaissance; a Madrid of the Muses and the Geniuses and one of the old-fashioned gossip corners; a Madrid which dreams of Goya and invents unique characters in the Rastro, or channels time and the wind through its beautiful gateways which do not open except to admit the visitor with generous, welcoming arms.

Ask, and each Madrilenian and each foreigner —what a silly thing to say; there is really no such thing as a foreigner, for as soon as the visitor comes to the city he becomes a part of it— will give a different version of what the city is to him.

Madrid is surrounded by a circle of extraordinary places and towns which seem to offer the secret to understanding the capital and at the same time they act as a complement to it. A water wheel, according to Lope de Vega himself, «where some people trail around others». For this reason, the visitor can do nothing better than lose himself in our city, drink its wines, discover its food, look at the heavens from time to time and then lower his view to the spires and weather vanes and its roof tops and garrets, with the flower pots filled with basel.

We have heard José del Corral speak of Madrid on many occasions and more than speak, he sings its praises, tours its streets and squares, followed by people who are anxious to discover why he knows so much about Madrid. We have seen him dismount like a village constable of olden times in order to complete his verbal enterprise by approaching the earth and the heart of this city. This book, in his hand, is something like a herald, a kettle-drum, a public decree posted on the street corner, something which we shall never forget.

José GARCIA NIETO
of the Spanish Royal Academy

Madrid monumental

1. Plaza Mayor. **2**. Ministerio de Asuntos Exteriores. **3**. Arco de Cuchilleros. **4**. Plaza de la Villa. Casa de Cisneros, Ayuntamiento, Torre de los Lujanes. **5**. Iglesia de San Pedro. **6**. Catedral de San Isidro. **7**. Monumento a Eloy Gonzalo. **8**. Mercado de la Cebada. **9**. La Fuentecilla. **10**. Iglesia de la Paloma. **11**. Puerta de Toledo. **12**. Iglesia de San Francisco el Grande. **13**. Iglesia de San Andrés. Capilla de San Isidro. **14**. Viaducto. **15**. Iglesia de la Almudena. **16**. Catedral de la Almudena. **17**. Iglesia de San Nicolás. **18**. Iglesia de Santiago. **19**. Teatro Real. **20**. Palacio Real. **21**. Convento de la Encarnación. **22**. Senado. **23**. Estación del Norte. **24**. Puente de Segovia. **25**. Ermita de San Antonio. **26**. Puerta del Sol. **27**. Iglesia de San Ginés. **28**. Convento de las Descalzas Reales. **29**. Iglesia del Carmen. **30**. Ministerio de Hacienda. **31**. Escuela de Bellas Artes de San Fernando. **32**. Iglesia de las Calatravas. **33**. Edificio «Metrópolis». **34**. Iglesia de San José. **35**. Banco de España. **36**. Congreso de los Diputados. **37**. Cámara de Comercio. **38**. Edificios en la calle de la Magdalena. **39**. Real Academia de la Historia. **40**. Convento e Iglesia de las Trinitarias. **41**. Fuente de Neptuno. **42**. Museo del Prado. **43**. Hospital de San Carlos. **44**. Estación de Atocha. **45**. Ministerio de Agricultura. **46**. Museo Etnológico. **47**. Observatorio Astronómico. **48**. Jardín Botánico. **49**. Retiro. Estatua del Angel Caído. **50**. Retiro. Palacio de Cristal. **51**. Retiro. Palacio de Velázquez. **52**. Retiro. Estanque. Monumento a Alfonso XII. **53**. Palacio de Comunicaciones. **54**. Fuente de Cibeles. **55**. La Bolsa. **56**. Real Academia de la Lengua. **57**. Museo del Ejército. **58**. Casón del Buen Retiro. **59**. Iglesia de los Jerónimos. **60**. Puerta de Alcalá. **61**. Iglesia de San Manuel y San Benito. **62**. Jardines del Descubrimiento. **63**. Monumento a Colón. **64**. Biblioteca Nacional y Museo Arqueológico. **65**. Palacio de Justicia e Iglesia de Santa Bárbara. **66**. Casa de las Siete Chimeneas. **67**. Convento de San Antón. **68**. Oratorio del Caballero de Gracia. **69**. Edificio de la Telefónica. **70**. Museo Municipal. **71**. Arco del 2 de Mayo. **72**. Iglesia de San Plácido. **73**. Iglesia Parroquial de San Martín. **74**. Convento de las Mercaderías. **75**. Palacio de la Prensa. **76**. Edificio «Callao». **77**. Cuartel del Conde Duque. **78**. Edificio España. **79**. Torre de Madrid. **80**. Plaza de España. Monumento a Cervantes. **81**. Templo de Debod.

Table of contents

Madrid, the capital

The Province and the Outskirts of the City

The gateways of Madrid

As a reminder of the times when Madrid was a fortified city, the Spanish capital still conserves today several old gateways which furnished once upon a time, access into the city. However, these gateways which the city has managed to conserve until our day are relatively modern for even the oldest ones are little more than two hundred years old. The other gateways, the real medieval ones, which formed part of the ancient ramparts, the Arab fortress which stood up against the continuous attacks of the Christian reconquerors or the posterior gateways which were put up by the new lords of the city, have since disappeared. Nothing remains of them other than, in some cases, their names.

The Gateways which still remain intact were part of a simple adobe wall, not a rampart of a fortified city, put up during the reign of Felipe IV at the beginning of the 17th century. Included within its perimeter was everything that is now considered the Center of Madrid. These walls, sections of which can still be seen closing off Retiro Park at Menéndez y Pelayo Street, served no other purpose than that of making it possible to supervise comings and goings into the city. In this way, arriving visitors were sure to pay the taxes levied on provisions and goods brought into the Spanish capital. These walls had a fiscal not a military value. Nevertheless, the people of Madrid tried to use its perimeter as a defense line for the City when the Napoleonic troops headed by the General himself, laid siege to the Court at the beginning of the 19th century. The stone and brick walls provided poor defense before the most powerful army of the epoch.

The registry clerks collected their corresponding duties and taxes at these walls whose beauty was enhanced in the 18th century under the reign of Carlos III, when handsome gateways were constructed around the perimeter. Unfortunately, of these artistic monuments only the Puerta de Alcalá remains which was, without a doubt, the most artistic.

The *Puerta de Alcalá* with its five arches, continues to decorate the graceful lines of the Calle Alcalá. It was the work of Sabbatini, the noted architect and engineer, whom Carlos III had brought with him from Naples, when he inherited the Spanish throne upon the unexpected death of his step-brother. Embedded columns,

⬆ The Puerta de Toledo Gateway.
⬅ One aspect of the Toledo Gateway.

↑ The Puerta de Alcalá Gateway.
← ☐ One aspect of the Alcalá Gateway.
→ An evening view.

chapters inspired by those of Michelangelo and sculptures by Robert Michel and Francisco Gutiérrez, beautifully adorn this Puerta. Construction on the Puerta de Alcalá was completed in 1778.

However, it should also be said that if the initial idea for the work was royal, the cost of its construction fell upon the shoulders of the Madrilenians, for the gateway was built with funds obtained from a tax levied on the wine sold in the City. Consequently, we might say we should thank the heaviest drinkers of old Madrid for their hearty contributions to the Puerta de Alcalá, a construction which graces and decorates Madrid today. Converted into an Arch of Triumph on the Calle de Alcalá, beside the recreational gardens which were initially designed for King Felipe IV in the 17th century, this gateway is indeed one of the most beautiful in

Europe and a source of pride to the Madrilenians.

The *Puerta de Toledo* is a more modern counterpart of the Puerta de Alcalá for it dates back to the beginning of the 19th century. Located at the end of the Calle Toledo, its foundations were laid with the intention of glorifying the ephemeral Spanish reign of Joseph Bonaparte. The brevity of his reign did not so much as allow time for the commencement of its

construction and work was naturally halted as a result of the vicissitudes of the War of Independence. When it was resumed, the final Arch was dedicated to King Fernando VII.

A heavier and less harmonious structure than the Puerta de Alcalá, the Puerta de Toledo opens its three arches in the direction of the river. Its mission has been reduced to that of a mere adornment, standing in the center of the plaza, crowned with a sculptural grouping by Salvatierra.

While the above-mentioned gateways were in fact used in their days as means of access into the Villa de Madrid, the same cannot be said for the *Puerta del Hierro* (Iron Gateway). This Gateway which now stands in the center of a small square in the middle of the La Coruña highway on the outskirts of Madrid appears to have stood at the entrance to the Royal Town of El Pardo.

Francisco Moradillo was the architect while the sculptural decoration can be attributed to Olivieri and the magnificent grille work to Francisco Barranco. Once again, Colmenar stone and granite were used with the addition of wrought iron, worked and twisted until it resembled fine lace.

Another elegant gateway stands at the entrance to the University City. It was put up in 1956, according to a project drawn up by architect López Otero, with reliefs by Moisés de la Huerta, keys by Ortells and finished off with a bronze chariot bearing the goddess Minerva, the work of the sculptor Aguirre.

↘ Moncloa. The Ministry.
← The Puerta de Hierro Gateway.
→ The Moncloa Arch.

Old Madrid

The grand metropolis of Madrid had its beginnings as a small village located on a natural ravine, overhanging the river, today's Calle de Segovia. A castle and sturdy ramparts were added to the small village, converting it into a fortified Arab town during the epoch of Arab domination under Caliph Muhamed V. The town attained its greatest level of growth many years later when, in 1561, Felipe II established the Villa de Madrid as the head of his Empire, which extended over two worlds. Madrid has been growing ever since, until it reached the size of the enormous city which we know today. However, even in the 17th century, under the reign of Felipe IV when the wall was put up to contain the city, Madrid had already achieved the perimeter which is today considered the Central District. Thus, we should consider this part

of town as Old Madrid: from the old boulevards to the Puerta de Toledo, from the Royal Palace to Retiro Park.

The most important historical structures are found in this area though many have since disappeared.

In view of the limited space which we have available here, we can only list the most interesting buildings and monuments for the visitor to

the «Very Noble, Loyal, Heroic, Imperial and Distinguished Village and Court of Madrid, Capital of Spain».

The *Plaza Mayor* is dominated by the austere design of the *Casa de la Panadería* (Bakery), reminiscent of the El Escorial Monastery and it was built in 1590 by architect Diego Sillero. It was years later, under the reign of Felipe III, that this building was taken as the main structure around which famed architect Juan Gómez de Mora designed and built the rest of the Plaza Mayor.

The Plaza Mayor was constructed with a dual purpose, that of serving as a market on week-days and as a theatre on important holidays and

↑ The Plaza Mayor. Casa de la Panadería (Bakery).
↘ One aspect of the Statue to Felipe III.
↩ One aspect of the facade of the Casa de la Panadería.
↪ The Plaza Mayor. An aerial view.

royal occasions. It fulfilled this mission for centuries. The Plaza Mayor has been throughout its history, a theatre, a field for royal jousting matches, a ring for bullfights, a site for public executions, a stage for the proclamation of a new king upon the death of the old, a place for the celebration of royal receptions and a religious station for processions and other solemnities.

In the center of the square is the statue of its creator, King Felipe III, the 17th century work of Italians Juan de Bolonia and Pedro de Tacca. The statue was finally erected in 1848 after it had stood in diverse locations throughout the city.

The original structure of the *Pontifical Basilica of San Miguel* (St. Michael's), the old parish church of San Justo, stands near Puerta Cerrada. The temple, of Italian lines and constructed in the 18th century, was one of the most beautiful examples of Italian Baroque in Madrid. It is the work of architects Bonavia and Rabaglio and is decorated with sculptures by Carisana and Miguel.

Surrounding this church are a set of narrow, winding streets, with steep climbs and several staircases, which lend a special charm to this corner of the city, enhanced still further by the blackened streetlamps which are fixed to the walls of the

ancient houses.

The present temple of *San Pedro el Viejo* (St. Peter's the Old), located at Calle del Nuncio, at the corner of Costanilla de San Pedro, is an old parish church whose tradition dates back to the year 1194. The one we can visit today was constructed in the 14th century and rebuilt in the 16th. Surviving from the primitive church is the beautiful, square Mudejar tower, which is one of the

oldest belltowers in Madrid.

The *Casa de Cisneros*, in the calle de Sacramento, now houses municipal offices but it still conserves much of its original interior and exterior splendor. It was constructed at the beginning of the 16th century by a nephew and heir of Cardinal Jiménez de Cisneros, who was the Regent of Spain upon the death of the Catholic Monarchs and until the arrival of Carlos I, nicknamed the Emperor.

Several rooms can be visited inside of Cisneros' Home to remind us of the magnificence of a bygone era. The *Salón de Tapices* (Tapistry Room) is decorated with excellent and highly valued 15th century

⬆ The Cuchilleros Arch.

↘ An old street-lamp.

⬅ A typical corner.

14

↑ The Plaza de la Villa.

→ ☐ Cisneros House. One aspect.

← The facade of the House of the Lujanes.

tapistries, woven with silk and wool threads. They are considered highly valuable pieces in view of their size and age. The room also conserves a beautiful coffered ceiling from its construction, which is the largest in Madrid. Other 17th century tapistries also from Brussels complete the magnificent decoration of what must have been the main drawing room of this mansion.

The *Plaza de la Villa* is an interesting urban grouping of old buildings in which the Tower of Los Lujanes stands out because of the date of its construction. The Tower is one of the few structures which Madrid still conserves from the end of the 15th, beginning of the 16th centuries.

Nearby is a Mudejar house which extends to the beginning of the Travesía del Cordón and which was home until this year to the

Municipal Periodical Library. It contains the beautiful Plateresque sepulcher of Francisco Ramírez, who was a general of the artillery forces under the Catholic Monarchs, as well as that of his wife, Beatriz Galindo, who was called «La Latina», because she was the knowledgeable teacher and friend of Queen Isabel I. These tombs were brought here when the Convent of Concepción Jerónima was

demolished in the last century. Francisco Ramírez and Beatriz Galindo were the founders of the Convent and though the religious structure no longer exists, it has left its name to the street where it once stood. Also in this house is the staircase which belonged to another building founded by the famous couple, the Hospital de La Latina, which was located at the Calle de Toledo. The Hospital had a Gothic

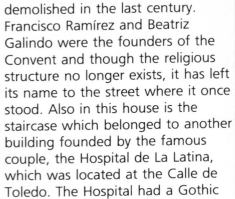

stone front, which is now found at the University City, near the School of Architecture. Both the beautiful staircase and the stone facade were the work of Moorish artist, Hazan, of whom we know very little.

However, the main building of the square is without a doubt, the Casa de la Villa, the home of the Madrid Town Council, with a small museum which can be visited. Juan Gómez de Mora designed the project for this building whose construction progressed slowly due to the economic penury of the City. It took, in fact, seventy-five years to build and it was not until 1696 that the finishing touches were added to the structure. Upon Gómez de Mora's death and after several other interventions, the building was

◥ Tower of Los Lujanes.
⬆ The dome of the San Isidro Chapel.
➡ The facade of the San Isidro Chapel.

The Basílica of San Miguel.

The Panecillo Passageway.

The Senate.

three tombs, in magnificent Plateresque style, appear in the Chapel and are certainly worthy of a visit, along with a look at the temple's magnificent main altar which is also Plateresque. The whole altar-piece and the tombs were the work of Francisco Giralte.

The *Church of San Andres* (St. Andre's) is one of the oldest and most venerated parish churches in Madrid and it is one of those mentioned in the 1202 Code of Laws of Madrid. However, the building existing today is really of more modern construction, for the previous Church of San Andrés was destroyed in the 17th century. One of the parishioners of this temple was the humble farmer, Isidro, who eventually became the Patron Saint of Madrid. He lived here in about the year 1000 and was buried in the small parish cemetery until his body was moved to the church for

veneration in the year 1212. He was canonized in 1625 and declared Patron Saint of the City though it is, nevertheless, true that the Saint was worshipped many centuries before.

In order to exhibit the remains of San Isidro to the Madrilenians, the

finally completed by Teodoro de Ardemans, who gave it its definitive exterior appearance and the decorative coats of arms and the carved doorways. Tapistries, sculptures, paintings, 18th century lamps, from the Royal Factory of La Granja, fine crystal, porcelain and other important pieces make up the decoration of the reception halls of the Casa de la Villa, which the tourist in Madrid will certainly enjoy

visiting.

Near the Town Council is another interesting group of buildings located near the Carrera de San Francisco and made up of the Plazas of La Paja, los Carros and San Andrés.

At the highest point of the Plaza de la Paja, near what was once the palace of one of the oldest families in Madrid, the Vargas family, is the *Chapel of the Bishop,* known thusly in Madrid and in Art History, despite the fact that its real and liturgical name was Chapel of Santa María and San Juan de Letrán.

Bishop Gutierre de Vargas Carvajal founded the Chapel at the beginning of the 16th century and its construction, still of Gothic style, was intented for the burial of the founder and his parents, Francisco de Vargas, an important member of the Court of the Catholic Monarchs, and his wife, Isabel de Vargas. The

◥ The Bishop's Chapel.
✝ The Convent of the Encarnación.
▭ Monument to Lope de Vega.
▭ Convent of the Encarnación. The facade.

18

Chapel of San Isidro was built beside the Church of San Andrés. The Chapel was destroyed in 1936 but has undergone considerable reconstruction since that date. Pedro de la Torre designed the project in 1642 and the square chapel was constructed beneath a graceful dome which conserves all of its exterior beauty. It had a very impressive interior and above the central altar was a silver urn —a gift from the Madrid silversmith guild at the beginning of the 17th century— to house the mummified body of the Saint. St. Isidro's remains are now found in Madrid's provisional Cathedral, located in the Calle Toledo. This building originally belonged to the Imperial College of the Company of Jesus, founded in 1599 by Juana de Austria, the daughter of Emperor Carlos V of Germany and the I of the Spain. The Imperial College was very influential

in the country's cultural life during the so-called Century of Gold.

The church, which is today a Cathedral, was constructed by the Jesuit Father Francisco Bautista. The fact that Madrid was dependent on the very large Toledo Diocese, is the reason why the capital never had its own Cathedral like the other Castilian cities. When the Madrid-Alcalá Diocese was established in the middle of the 19th century, a

Cathedral seat was required and this temple, of huge proportions, was selected. Ever since, attempts have been continually made to furnish Madrid with a proper Cathedral and construction was begun on one near the Royal Palace, initiated by the Marquis of Cubas and reformed in an aesthetic sense by architects Chueca and de Miguel in our days. Only the crypt of this Cathedral has been completed though there is a

strong local movement focused on concluding the construction within the next few years.

The *Temple of San Francisco el Grande,* opposite the beginning of the Carrera de San Francisco, deserves not only an unrushed visit but also an explanation of its existence and its vicissitudes.

Several important Madrilenian monasteries had existed during the Middle Ages. The first church which was surely Gothic disappeared in the 18th century and construction on the present one was soon initiated. Despite the existence of several projects prepared by such great architects as Ventura Rodríguez and Hermosilla, the one drawn up by a Franciscan brother,

◣ One aspect of the San Isidro, facade.

↑ The Puerta Cerrada Square.

◄ The Cathedral of San Isidro.

⬆ San Francisco el Grande Church.

⬅☐ The Little Fountain.

⬅ Church of La Paloma.

Francisco Cabezas, was preferred.

In 1781, the six side chapels and the main altar were decorated with some fine paintings and by seven of the most important painters of the Court, each of whom was given a specific theme in the way of an artistic contest. Tha magnificent painter Francisco de Goya was among the artists selected.

In 1860, Cánovas del Castillo wanted to furnish the church with a

lavish decoration. Of the seven paintings which had initially adorned the church, three were moved to the first chapel as we enter on the right and another three were placed to the left. The seventh painting which had corresponded to the main altar was hung on the stairway leading to the Choir. Goya's canvas is the one in the center of the first chapel on our left.

The paintings entirely cover the domes and walls, producing a great impression on the visitor.

Madrid's history records several projects to build a *viaduct* to span the Calle de Segovia, some of which date back to the first years of the 19th century. However, the first Viaduct was not constructed until 1874. It was replaced by another in 1942, which successive reformations and consolidations have helped to maintain until the present day.

The *Vistillas of San Francisco* offer an interesting balcony over the Madrid landscape and it was the setting for summer festivals and *verbenas* with the stunning backdrop of the landscape of the other side of the Manzanares.

We should now refer to other buildings of interest which are not far from the quarter we are visiting. Here we will find the *Plaza de Provincia* and the *Ministry of Foreign Affairs*.

The building housing the Foreign Affairs Ministry was built in the 17th century by the Marquis Crescenci, the same author of the Royal Pantheon of the Monastery of El Escorial and it was intended as the City Courthouse and Jail.

Before we reach the Royal Palace, we should make two more stops on either side of the Plaza de Oriente: the Church of Santiago and the Convent of La Encarnación.

The *Church of Santiago* replaced another temple and it was built in 1811 in accordance with the plans of architect Cuervo.

Much more interesting will prove a visit to the *Convent of la Encarnacion,* founded by Felipe III and Queen Margarita in order to commemorate the expulsion of the Moors from Spain.

⬆ Viaduct over Segovia Street.

⬊ Plaza de Ramales.

⬅ Church of Santiago.

⬆ Ministry of Foreign Affairs.

⬅⬜ One aspect of the Ministry.

⬅ The Santa Cruz Tower.

↑ Plaza de la Armería (Armory Square).

→ Street-lamp of the Plaza de Oriente.

→ An aerial view of the Royal Palace.

↓ The fountain of the Campo del Moro.

The Royal Palace

The Arabs had chosen the same spot where the Royal Palace stands today as the site for their castle. The Moors made Madrid the watchtower for the protection of the City of Toledo, which was the head of the Arab kingdom, against possible attacks coming from the Christian armies located on the other side of the mountains.

The old Arab Alcázar, after the reconquest, was re-conditioned as a

royal residence. When Madrid was selected Capital of the Kingdom by Felipe II, the Palace was considered the official royal residence though the King would in truth spend more time in the Monastery of El Escorial, a day's journey away. It became the official residence of the two Felipes, the III and the IV. Diego de Velázquez lived and painted here as well. At the end of the reign of the House of Austria with Carlos II, the

first Bourbon King, Felipe V, lived here upon his arrival in Madrid until Christmas eve of 1734 when a fire put an end to the Arab castle, which had been modernized by the Christians Fortunately, some of the many great works of art could be saved from the fire.

Felipe V wanted the new palace to be constructed on the precise spot of the old, despite its rugged and steep location and this made

construction difficult and expensive. In accordance with the royal instructions, Juan Bautista Sachetti carried out the project with just a few minor modifications. Facades 131 meters long mark the limits of the granite and white stone structure, which is one of the most beautiful royal residences in Europe. The first stones was set in place in 1738 but the Palace could not be inhabited until the times of Carlos III, in 1764.

An equestrian statue of Felipe IV stands in the center of the Plaza del Oriente, the work of Pedro de Tacca. The king wanted his horse to appear rearing up, with its front legs in the air. This made it necessary to calculate the hollow

⬆ The Royal Palace. Carlos III room.

↘ Facade facing the Plaza de Oriente.

⬅ Ceilings of the Gasparini room.

⬆ The Royal Palace seen from the Campo del Moro.

⬅ Sabatini Gardens.

made a wooden bust of the King. The bust, together with a portrait painted by Velázquez, were sent to Florence so that the Italian artist could carry out the commission of Cosme de Medici, who wanted to present the finished work to the King as a gift.

Very close to the Plaza de Oriente is the Plaza de Ramales and it was here in the Church of San Juan that Velázquez was buried. The remains of the famous painter were lost along with the Church and today a monolith stands to mark the general area as Velázquez's final resting place.

Beautiful, romantic street-lamps illuminate the Square and are faithful copies of those which existed in the times of King Fernando VII. Behind the Place is the Campo del Moro or Palace Park, a group of gardens whichs can be visited.

The Royal Palace, which is magnificently furnished, with one of the most important tapistry collections in the world and excellent paintings from different epochs —including several by Goya— is a highly interesting museum complex which should not be missed. Worthy of special attention are the Throne Room, covered with red fabric and ceilings painted by Bayeu; the Gasparini Room, with lovely Chinese stucco work; the Porcelain Room of the Buen Retiro factory, decorated with very fine porcelain plaques; the Carlos III Room, covered with light blue silk, as the habit of his Order; the Salon of Mirrors and many other rooms containing lavish furnishings and magnificent paintings.

In addition, the Carriage collection, the Tapistry display, the Pharmacy, the Library and the very important Armory are independent museums within the complex which represent very interesting visits.

In the Plaza de Oriente, opposite the Palace, construction on the Royal Theatre was begun in 1818 and completed in 1850. It was closed for urgent repairs in 1925 and was reopened as a concert hall in 1966.

and filled parts of the sculpture carefully so that the piece could maintain this position. It is said that Galileo himself was the one to make the calculations. In order to give the statue the required resemblance to the monarch, the magnificent sculptor from Sevilla, Martínez Montañés, the artist who created the fine imagery of Seville's Easter *pasos* (platforms bearing sculptures representing the Passion of Christ)

◥ Cathedral of the Almudena. Rear facade.
◥ Cathedral of the Almudena. Main facade.
◄ The Royal Palace seen from the Plaza de Oriente.

↑ The Royal Theatre.

↔☐ Plaza de Oriente. Statue of Felipe IV.

↔ The stage of the Royal Theatre.

The shores of the Manzanares

Manzanares, «a stream in apprenticeship as a river», in the words of a classic writer, has been the object of jeers and taunts from the oldest and most modern writers. Its shallow waters, which were always more abundant in the sub-soil than above the sandy bed, made the Manzanares more of an invisible river, especially when the summer heat dried its surface waters. Nevertheless, the Manzanares was capable of causing great floods like the one which washed away the original Toledo bridge from its very foundation. As a result, a narrow wooden footwalk was erected and stood until the 18th century when the City Magistrate, the Marquis of Vadillo, commissioned Ribera to build the beautiful, ornate bridge which is used today.

The Manzanares River can actually be said to run through Madrid at

the point where it passes below the spans of the *San Fernando Bridge.* The bridge was constructed by Fernando VI in the 18th century to facilitate the passing of the royal retinue to El Pardo and in memory of the King and his wife, we find the images of their Patron Saints, San Fernando and Santa Bárbara. The river is then channelled through a special section, as it flows around the capital. The very first efforts at canalization have long been forgotten but it was followed by another which is now undergoing major reforms.

One of the important buildings which faces the river as it flows past the urban center is the Sanctuary of the Virgen del Puerto, the first work of the great 18th century Baroque architect, Pedro de Ribera, who was commissioned by the afore-mentioned City Magistrate, the Marquis de Vadillo.

Next comes the *Segovia Bridge* , of austere, clear and bare design; it can only be praised for the beauty of its dimensions. The bridge was built in the 16th century by Juan de Herrera and it conserves all of the controlled force of his Escorial

↑ Sanctuary of the Virgen del Puerto.
↖ The Manzanares river.
↩ The Toledo Bridge.
→ The Segovia Bridge.

Monastery/Palace. In the past, these shores were used as public washing places, where the sun whitened and dried the underclothing of the Madrilenians.

The waters of the Manzanares also bathe the *Pradera de San Isidro* (Meadow), a scene which was so masterfully immortalized in a delightful painting by Goya. Behind the meadow, the vertical lines of the cypress trees mark the presence of the old romantic cemeteries of Madrid: San Isidro, Santa María, San Justo...

When passing near the Campo del Moro, the river slows down as it reaches the outskirts of what was the «Quinta del Sordo», the last residence of Francisco de Goya in Madrid and the Sanctuary of San Antonio de la Florida. Here is one of the key points on our visit to Madrid, for we should stop to admire the frescoes painted by Goya on the walls of the Sanctuary which today houses the painter's own tomb.

We must still stop at the Sanctuary of San Isidro, a place famous for the solemn devoutness of the *romería* (pilgrimage) and the uproar and gaiety of its *verbena* (traditional, open-air dance).

Then, our river flows below the ornately decorated *Toledo Bridge*. Another magnificent structure credited to Pedro de Ribera, it has niches in the center of its roadway which house the limestone-carved statues of San Isidro and his wife, Santa María de la Cabeza, the work of sculptor Ron.

The river still has to cross below the cement arches of the *Puente de la Princesa* . The Princesa bridge standing today is the second to be named thusly. It was built in 1929 to replace the previous one which

dated back to the beginning of the century and was dedicated to the then Princess of Asturias. It was a metallic structure reminiscent of the first bridges which were constructed for railway crossings.

The Manzanares flows near the Arganzuela Park, whose principal monument is the huge fountain and its Obelisk, topped with a metallic North Star. This is the same obelisk which presided over the old fountain which once stood in the center of the Plaza de Roma, also called Manuel Becerra Square.

At this point the river returns to its country setting and fields and trees sprout up along its shores. The constructions grow scarce and the countryside, the old Madrid countryside, forms the backdrop for the Manzanares once again.

◥ The Norte (North) Station.

✝ San Antonio de la Florida. Museum.

← San Antonio de la Florida.

⊞ The Rosaleda Rose Garden in the Oeste Park.

⊞ ☐ Fountain in the Rosaleda.

⊞ The Manzanares river.

The center of town

There are still many more jewels in Madrid which we have not yet covered. In the very heart of the city, we will find old churches, ancient monasteries, artistic fountains and extraordinary buildings which should be mentioned, if only in passing.

San Ginés, in Arenal Street, is an old church which has undergone many transformations over the centuries. Old images, some of which enjoyed great veneration in other epochs, adorn the altars but San Ginés has a special jewel, its Chapel of Christ, belonging to the Congregation of the *Esclavos del Santo Cristo*. It is a tiny, beautiful church, with bronzes by Pompeyo Leoni, paintings by Francisco Ricci, sculptures by Vergaz and Nicolo Fumo and even one of the most precious versions of «Christ throwing the merchants out of the Temple», by El Greco (this is one of

the few paintings by El Greco which can be found in Madrid outside of the city's museums).

The *Descalzas Reales,* an ancient palace converted into a monastery, is a magnificent complex of artistic wealth. Part Museum belonging to the National Patrimony, the Descalzas Reales is open to the public on certain days and the rooms where the professed nuns live in the strictest enclosure can be visited.

It is not surprising that the visitor to Madrid will frequently ask why the Puerta del Sol is named «Door of the Sun». A gateway once stood here as part of the wall which enclosed the small town of Madrid, existing before the 16th century. And this Gateway —like so many others built throughout Spain— had a sun carved on it. Thus it lent its name to a square which has conserved it for over four centuries, long after the original gate and wall have disappeared.

Among the many Madrid theatres, special mention should be made of the Teatro Español, heir to the old Corral del Príncipe, which stood on the same spot and in

⊕ Church of San Ginés.
◺ Convent of the Descalzas.
⬌ Tower of San Ginés.
⬌ Puerta del Sol.

which plays by the writers of the *Siglo del Oro* (Golden Age) were put on. Also worthy of citing is the Teatro de la Zarzuela, built for the presentation of *zarzuelas* (light operettas) by a group of 19th century theatre-lovers —authors and composers— and several bankers.

The Congress building was another structure built during the reign of Isabel II with sculptures by Ponciano Ponzano. A statue of

Cervantes stands before the Congress and it was the first statue to be put up in Madrid to a person who was not of royal blood.

And close by is what remains of the Monastery of San Jerónimo, which underwent great reforms. It was founded during the times of Enrique IV, at the beginning of the 15th century near the Manzanares river and it was moved to this spot by the Catholic Monarchs.

The Fountain of Neptune stands between the Congress and the Monastery of Los Jerónimos and corresponds to a series of reforms on the Paseo del Prado, undertaken by Carlos III and begun at Atocha, with the *La ALcachofa* (Artichoke) fountain (today standing in Retiro Park). The work on the Paseo continued with four identical fountains located near the Museum, the work of Robert Michel, and was followed by the Neptune fountain,

built by Juan Pascual de Mena, the Apolo fountain, by Vergaz, and Cibeles by Francisco Gutiérrez and Robert Michel. Thus was the solemn design of the old Paseo del Prado which was very much in vogue during the last century.

The *Bolsa* (Stock Market) building standing on the Paseo del Prado, was built in this century by architect Repullés, with a large arcaded colonnade. Of similar design is the

nearby Bank of Spain of practically the same period, a beautiful building by Lastra, which has undergone many expansions.

We do not want to neglect to mention, among other places, two

⬓ Royal Language Academy.

⬓ Zarzuela Theatre.

⬒ Congress.

⬄ Teatro Español.

↑ Neptuno Square and the Church of the Hieronymites.

← ☐ Neptune Fountain.

→ Facade of the Church of the Hieronymites.

which is a magnificent architectural structure built by Antonio Palacios. Due to its Cathedral-like appearance, it is often called «Our Lady of the Communications».

Beside the Palace is the Banco de España, a fine building with a magnificent collection of paintings including several canvases by Goya. On the other side of the Calle Alcalá is the Palacio de Buenavista, today headquarters for the Army Chiefs of

Staff. The palace was originally built by the Duke and Duchess of Alba on what was the orchard of Juan Fernández.

The last building on the square is the Palace of the Marqueses de Linares, today housing a credit company.

On the right of Cibeles, is the Salón del Prado and on the left is the paseo de Recoletos. It is named for the Convent of the Augustine Recollets which was located more or less where the National Library stands today.

Today gay outdoor cafes preside over Recoletos, such as the Café Gijón, with its literary tradition, and the Teide.

interesting churches. One is the Church and Convent of Santa Ana, of which only the name on the Square remains, and which stood opposite the Teatro Español. The other church, of San Manuel and San Benito, was a modern work by Arbos, a constitutional temple which according to the taste of the period was put up in a more or less Byzantine style.

In the Calle Alcalá, is the temple which once belonged to the Convent of the Comendadoras de Calatrava, who came to Madrid in the 17th century. The remains of the Convent underwent considerable alteration when the building was reconstructed during the last century.

This section of the Calle de Alcalá was even in the 17th century more of a road than a street. There were a few private homes which stood among the many convents which

have long since disappeared: the Convents of the Calatravas, the Vallecas, the Nuns of Pinto, the Baronesas, the Carmelitas Descalzas...

The Plaza de Cibeles is today one of the nerve centers of Madrid, where many public transport lines, both surface and underground, have their terminals. Many important buildings are located here as well, such as the Communications Palace

◥ Church of San José.
◥ Church of San Manuel and San Benito.
⬆ The Stock Market.

⬆ The Alcalá Gateway and Street.

◼︎◻︎ Bank of Spain.

◼︎ A night-time view of the Cibeles fountain.

◼︎ Communications Palace. Cibeles Square.

The Prado Museum

Any attempt to cover in the brief space of a publication of this nature, the contents of the Prado Museum, even in a highly summarized version, is an impossible task, for we are talking about one of the best art collections in the whole world. We will merely make mention of some of the Museum's more outstanding characteristics.

Let us begin with the building. As we often do not see the forest for the trees, the paintings frequently

do not allow us the opportunity to admire their packaging. Nevertheless, the museum building is truly exceptional. It is one of the best works of the great Neo-classic architect Juan de Villanueva who was commissioned by Carlos III to build a Natural Science Museum and a Research Center for this specialty.

In truth, the royal idea was well-conceived and was very much in keeping with the cultural concept of

the times: A Botanical Garden and beside it, a building to house the collections and promote the study and teaching of these sciences. However, after its construction, the building was never occupied. It was almost destroyed during the French invasion and the lead from its roof was used in the making of cannon balls.

After the war, King Fernando VII wanted to display the magnificent royal art collections, which dated back to the times of the Catholic Monarchs, to the public and he proposed the creation of the Painting Museum, using the hitherto unused building.

A long line of monarchs had succeeded to the Spanish throne, all of whom were fortunately art lovers: all the kings of the House of Austria and those of the Bourbons, up until the very founder of the art museum. Thus, the initial collection of the Prado was abundant and highly varied. It was expanded over the years with paintings proceeding from the convents which disappeared during the period of Disentailment of the ecclesiastic

⬆ The northern facade of the Museum.

↘ Statue of Goya.

➡ Velázquez. *Las Meninas*

↑ Spanish Picture Gallery.
→□ Velázquez. *Las Lanzas.*
→ One aspect of the Gallery.

properties in the past century.

In this manner, a unique and magnificent collection of artwork of incalculable importance was brought together.

Rubens, who had spent lengthy periods of time in Spain, is also well-represented in the Museum, not to mention the work of just about every major Spanish painter.

The Prado Museum assembles the only complete collection of works by Velázquez, capable of making us understand the painter's art. El Greco has just as many paintings here as in his hometown of Toledo where he lived, painted and died.

As for Goya, we can say that the Prado has the greatest ensemble of his works to illustrate his genius and style, such as the black paintings and his truly unique sketches for the royal tapistries.

The rich collection of sculptures grows pale in comparison with so much pictorial abundance, though there are several truly fine pieces. We should add that all of the paintings which are on exhibit in the Prado belong to the Museum, whose collections were never enriched by illegal confiscations or spoils of war, as has been the case with other museums in the world.

We wish to bring the visitor's attention to the set of primitive paintings, proceeding from ancient altar-pieces, which have been acquired by the Museum, either as a whole or as separate panels or fragments. There is also an important collection of Italian paintings for which the works by Raphael stand out and among other masterpieces, the exceptional «Tránsito de la Virgen» by Mantegna.

This enormous museum is expanded still further by the *Casón del Buen Retiro,* which is close-by. Originally the huge dance hall of the no longer existent palace, the building now houses Picasso's well-known canvas «The destruction of Guernica», which became especially famous for ultra-artistic reasons.

The visitor should keep in mind that the Museum must be the object of repeated visits, for he or she will make endless discoveries which cannot possibly be enumerated in so few lines.

↘ Statue of Velázquez.

↘ Main facade of the Museum.

↑ Zurbarán. Visión de San Pedro Nolasco

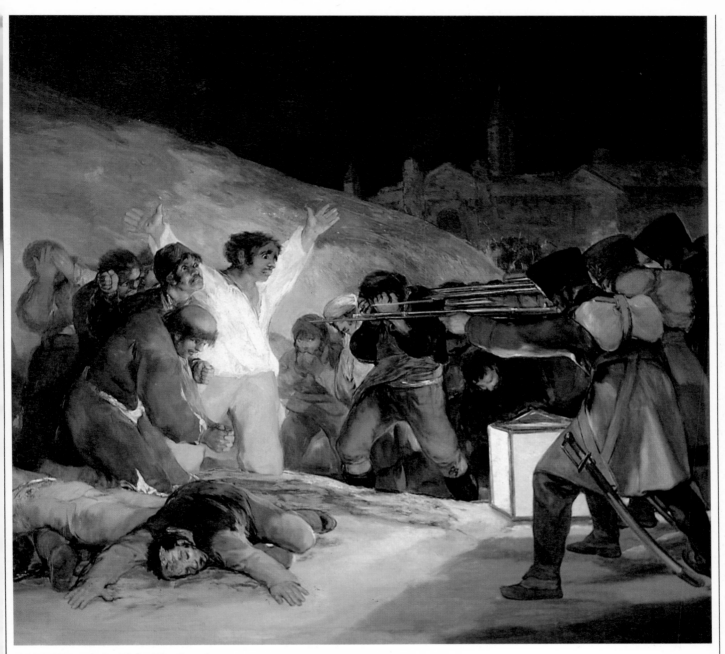

↑ Goya. *Fusilamientos del 2 de Mayo.*

→ ☐ El Greco. *Caballero de la mano en el pecho.*

← Goya. *El Quitasol.*

Retiro Park and the Botanical Gardens

In order to understand *Retiro Park,* we must go back to the very beginning of the 17th century when it was first created, though its construction was completed in 1635. At that time the only building standing amidst the fields in that part of town was the Convent of San Jerónimo el Real.

Felipe II had several rooms constructed in the Monastery, which he used during periods of mourning

and Lent. He made good use of these lodgings because of the death of many of his loved ones. For this reason, it was known as His Majesty's Retreat *(Retiro)* or simply, El Retiro. When the Count-Duke of Olivares, Gaspar de Guzmán —of whom Velázquez painted a magnificent portrait which hangs in the Prado— decided to build a palace for his lord, Felipe IV, he thought that that spot was ideal. He

began by purchasing the land and then ordered the construction of a palatial complex. From that architectural grouping, only the Army Museum and the Casón del Buen Retiro remain today.

The present Army Museum was one of the bays which was surrounded by several patios making up part of the Palace. The *Salón de los Reinos* —within the Army Museum and decorated along the

cornice with the coats of arms of all of the kingdoms dependent upon the Spanish crown— was the Throne Room of the Palace for which Velázquez painted «La Rendición de Breda» (The Surrender of Breda). This famous work was commissioned by the King and is exhibited today in the Prado Museum along with the equestrian portraits of Felipe III and Felipe IV as well as of their wives, and the Monarchs' son, Prince Baltasar Carlos.

Behind the Museum were the large gardens, a huge lake —it is now part of the Park— and many little sanctuaries scattered throughout the property, none of which have been able to survive to

⬆ An aerial view of the Lake.

↘ Calle Alfonso XII.

⬅ The Tritones fountain.

⬆ The Alfonso XII Monument.

⬅☐ One aspect of the Alfonso XII Monument.

⬅ One aspect of the lions on the pier.

47

our day. But we should mention that the Retiro of Felipe IV was indeed larger than the one we know today, for it also included the property which extended between the Park and the Prado, from Atocha to Cibeles. For this reason, the old palace or what remains of it, is now located outside of the gardens in an enormous section of land which a Town Council needy of funds and short on scruples sold off indiscriminately.

There still exist copies of an old map of Madrid, sketched house by house, in 1652, by a Portuguese cartographer —at that time, Portugal was part of the Spanish Crown— which enable us to appreciate the original size of the Park.

The Court of Felipe IV was a gay court under a poet king and Retiro was the ideal setting for the resplendent parties and theatrical

plays, some of which were performed on stages floating on the lake or from the tiny island which stood in its center. We know that the King and his party watched the performances from boats.

Those plays for the Court, which were also attended by the townsfolk, scored great triumphs for Lope de Vega, Tirso de Molina, Calderón de la Barca, Quiñones de Benavente, de Villamediana and so

many other authors of that great century for the Spanish Letters.

Once the building of the present Royal Palace was completed, the popularity of the Retiro began to diminish. The new dynasty had created the gardens of La Granja and Aranjuez and El Retiro was no longer fashionable.

It was then ceded to the Madrid Town Council and it eventually became one of the most beautiful

urban parks, set within the very heart of the city.

An extended municipal policy filled it with a series of monuments the most famous and the largest of which is certainly the one dedicated to Alfonso XII, which stands at the site of the old royal pier. The work, by a variety of architects and sculptors, like all collective works, shows the effects of an imbalance but it is nevertheless, impressive and decorative.

Palaces were also constructed for exhibitions, one of which is of special interest, the Palacio de Cristal. An old greenhouse, built for the display of exotic plants, the Crystal Palace is an iron structure of fine style and magnificent

↩ The Rosaleda rose garden.
↗ The Lake beside the Palacio de Cristal.
↓ Retiro fountain.

↑ The Crystal Palace.
⬅☐ The Velázquez Palace.
➡ The Fisherman's Cottage.

proportions, the work of architect Velázquez Bosco, who was also the author of the nearby Velázquez Palace, intended as well for exhibitions. The Palacio de Velázquez was constructed for an Exhibition of Philippine products, when the Philippines were still a Spanish territory.

The Porcelain Factory was founded by Carlos III in El Retiro in the 18th century and it produced magnificent works, some of which are on display in the Municipal Museum. The English, Spain's allies against the French invaders, destroyed the Factory because they feared the competition for the production of their own porcelain factories.

And a final mention should be made of the monuments to Cajal and Pérez Galdós, both the work of Victorio Macho.

At the end of the Paseo del Prado, between the Prado Museum and Atocha is the *Botanical Gardens.* Fernando VI had already created a similar institution at Soto de Migas Calientes but Carlos III moved the Gardens here in 1781. It is surrounded by a magnificent iron gate, with several entrances.

The Botanical Gardens took on scientific importance from the very beginning and the King sent several expeditions to different parts of the world in order to collect specimens and reproduce others in drawings for this collection.

Different statues have been distributed throughout the area which remember the Garden's founders as well as great Spanish botanists of different epochs. They brighten the beautiful Gardens which apart from their scientific and scholarly worth also serve the double function of amusement and relaxation.

The renewing of an old Botanical Garden tradition has been announced, that of giving medicinal herbs free to those who request them to cure their ailments. This old custom had been discontinued several years ago.

The drawings sketched by natives and by the members of the expedition headed by famous botanist Celestino Mutis, to Nueva Granada, are of exceptional value. There are more than 6,000 of them and they represent all the flora existing in that region when it still depended on the Spanish Crown. They are beautiful drawings which have only been reproduced in part by a magnificent edition intended as a collector's item for bibliophiles, due to its characteristics and price.

A statue stands in the center of the square, between the Prado Museum and the Botanical Gardens, dedicated to the great Spanish painter Bartolomé Esteban Murillo, the work of sculptor Sabino Medina under commission to the Seville Town Countil. The Madrid Town Council asked Seville for a reproduction of the statue which was placed here close to where many of Murillo's paintings are on exhibit.

◥ Monument to Carlos III in the Botanical Gardens.

⊟ Main facade of the Gardens (Villanueva Gateway).

⬆ Plaza de Carlos V and the Paseo del Prado.
⬅⬜ Ministry of Agriculture.
⬅ Plaza de Carlos V. San Carlos Hospital.

Other buildings and places of interest

The broad Plaza de Atocha spreads out after the Botanical Gardens and the square is today covered by a great network of overhead highways to facilitate the movement of the dense traffic in the area.

The old railway station, known as the *Estación de Mediodía*, is located here, of iron work architecture, opposite which is the building housing the Ministry of Agriculture.

Architect Velázquez Bosco put up the structure, which was intended to lodge the Ministry of Public Works and Economy.

This area is pending re-development, when the station will no longer provide railway service but the building will be conserved whatever its destination.

One of the gateways of Madrid's old ramparts stood here. It was the Puerta de Atocha or Las

Campanillas, which left the old Monastery of Las Campanillas outside of the city limits. From here the wall extended to Retiro and the Puerta de Alcalá and then to Recoletos until it reached the Plaza de Colón where the Gardens of the *Descubrimiento* (Discovery) are now found. The huge stone structures commemorating Columbus' adventure and facing the Calle Serrano are the modern work of

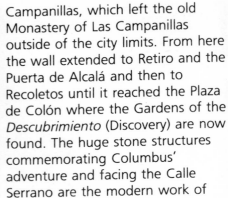

Vaquero. There is also a statue to Columbus by Suñol which stands on an elevated pedestal done by Melida, overlooking the gardens and one of the City's newest Cultural Centers. Across the street is Jareño's huge building which houses the National Library and the Archaeological Museum.

The National Library is another source of pride to Spaniards for it contains extensive collections of old books, manuscripts, engravings, maps, etc.

The wall continued from Colón —where the Recoletos wall stood— along what was the old Madrid boulevards which have unfortunately disappeared in order to make way for Madrid's pressing traffic. The next gateway stood at

← Alcalá Street and the Gran Vía.

↘ Paseo de Recoletos (Mariblanca fountain).

↑ Paseo del Prado (Apollo fountain).

52

↑ Gran Vía. Plaza del Callao.
↔ □ The Metropolis building.
↔ The Gran Vía at night.

53

today's Plaza de Santa Bárbara, called thusly because of the Convent of this order. Nearby is the Palace of Justice, built in this century and near it, the Church of Santa Bárbara, which had nothing to do with the no longer existent Convent. The Church was founded by Fernando VI's wife —Bárbara de Braganza— in the 18th century. The couple are buried in this temple and they were among the few monarchs who were not buried in El Escorial. The tomb of Fernando VI is a beautiful monument located to the right in the Church's transept, the work of sculptor Francisco Gutiérrez.

The wall continued along the boulevards, today the streets of Sagasta, Carranza, Alberto Aguilera, with the gateway at Pozos de la Nieve (today, the Glorieta de Bilbao) and the Gateway of San Bernardo or Fuencarral.

Near the first of the above-

mentioned gateways, in Fuencarral Street, is the Municipal Museum, installed in an old building constructed in the 18th century by Pedro de Ribera. It is well worth the visit because of the many souvenirs and historical pieces which tell the story of an old Madrid. In the gardens behind the Museum is a Baroque fountain which was carved by Ribera for placement in Antón Martín Square. It was moved from

one place to another until it was finally set up on the Museum grounds.

The Parque del Oeste is near the point where Alberto Aguilera and the Calle Princesa meet and it was created at the beginning of the century by Mayor Alberto Aguilera. It has many charming corners and installed at one end of the park is the magnificent Temple of Debod. The Temple, which was built during

the times of the Pharoahs, stood on Elephantine Island and was brought over from Egypt as a gift to the Spanish government for their help in saving many of the Egyptian artistic treasures. A key figure in that project was famous archaeologist Martín Almagro. The main thoroughfare of the Parque del Oeste is the well known Paseo de Rosales with its charming views of the river and landscape beyond.

If we continue along the Calle de la Princesa, which is today like Madrid's Latin Quarter, due to the proximity of the University City, we come to the Palacio de Liria, built in the 18th century. It is filled with an extraordinary variety of artistic treasures, among which we can

⬆ Church of Las Calatravas.

↘ A bank.

⬅ The Arch of the Dos de Mayo.

⬆ Church of Santa Bárbara.

⬅⬜ Colón Square. National Library.

⬅ One view of the Monument to Columbus.

- ⬆ Debod Temple.
- ⬌ Monument to Cervantes.
- ⬌☐ Plaza de España.
- ⬇ Building on Ferraz street.

single out the works by Francisco de Goya. The Dukedom of Liria became part of the House of Alba and now the Duke and Duchess of Alba —who possess some thirty other titles— live in this Palace and its ample gardens today.

The Calle Princesa reaches the Plaza de España, a huge square surrounded by tall buildings —the work of Otamendi— in the center of which is the monument dedicated to Miguel de Cervantes. The figures of his famous characters, Don Quixote and Sancho Panza, form the front part of this classic Madrid monument.

Behind the España Building is the interesting Church of San Marcos, with an oval design, the 18th century work of Ventura Rodríguez.

The Plaza de España closes off one end of the busy Gran Vía which has its beginnings at the corner of the Calle de Alcalá, near Cibeles.

Modern streets, lined with some rather mediocre buildings, offer, nevertheless, a great deal of commercial activity and entertainment possibilities.

We must make mention of another quarter, not quite on our route which has become especially popular with the younger generations: the Maravillas or Malasaña quarter.

This quarter is centered around the Plaza del Dos de Mayo (Second of May), heroically defended by the Madrilenians against the invasion of the Napoleonic troops. The quarter is made up of generally narrow streets whose houses for the most part were built in the 19th century though some of those still standing date back to the 18th. The advanced age of the buildings and their relative lack of comfort have made many of their original dwellers

abandon them for more modern homes. These rudimentary apartments were then occupied by young people, students, for the most part, who found cheap lodging in the center of Madrid and who did not mind the absence of elevators and bathrooms. The existence of this new class of residents gave birth to new taverns, bars and restaurants —many with foreign sounding names—. Thus, a new Madrilenian quarter was formed which soon earned a bad reputation, for its frequent drug traffic.

⬆ Parque del Oeste.
↘ Parque of San Isidro.
⬅ Monument to Princess Isabel.

58

⬆ Princesa Street.

⬌▢ Plaza de España.

⬌ Casón del Buen Retiro museum.

The Madrid Museums

The fame and significance of the Prado Museum collection tends to overshadow the remaining Madrid Museums. Certainly none of them can match the importance of the Prado but the city's museums do have valuable collections and interesting presentations.

Next, on the list after the Prado is the *Fine Arts Museum* of the San Fernando Academy, housed in the old Palace of Goyeneche at Alcalá Street. The Museum is made up of works which were presented by their authors upon their admittance into the Academy. Other works came from Convents and Churches during the Disentailment and still others were the product of different donations and purchases. Several important canvases by Goya, Velázquez and other great painters make up the collection of this art gallery which was complemented with works from outstanding artists

of all epochs.

The *Lázaro Galdiano Museum* is a private foundation which was created by José Lázaro and his personal collections are exhibited in what was the art benefactor's own home, an attractive mansion located on the Calle de Serrano, corner of María de Molina. A variety of collections are on display: paintings, sculptures, imagery, weapons, furniture, porcelain, fabrics, crystal, clocks, fans, books, engravings, and a long list of additional items which cannot be listed here. There are even paintings by Goya and other major Spanish and foreign painters.

The *Army Museum,* near Calle Alfonso XII, occupies as we have said one of the few structures surviving from the old Retiro Palace. Uniforms and weapons used by the Spanish Army throughout its history are on display here, objects of historical value, such as the automobiles in which two Chiefs of State, General Prim and Eduardo Dato, were killed, an Arab room with an interesting collection of weaponry and fabrics, scale-models of fortifications and heavy artillery and even a room which displays a

⬆ Lázaro Galdiano Museum.

◣ Inside the Lazaro Galdiano Museum.

⬅ Casón del Buen Retiro Museum.

60

↑ The National Library.

↤ ☐ Stairway of the National Library.

↤ Museum of Decorative Arts.

The Municipal Museum also has scale reproductions of different important buildings, some of which are still existing today and others have long since disappeared. Many engravings, lithographs, a vast variety of objects, including the important collection of porcelain pieces from the Buen Retiro factory give us a more complete idea of our city's past.

Special mention should be made

huge collection of toy soldiers, all dressed up in period uniforms, depicting famous battles.

The *Archaeological* Museum, located behind the National Library, houses objects proceeding from different epochs, places and styles of art. The collection of Iberian objects and figurines are particularly interesting such as the classic Damas of Elche and Baza. The reproduction of the Altamira Cave should not be missed.

The *Municipal Museum* at Calle Fuencarral, number 78, has many very interesting objects and paintings which will enable the visitor to get to know Madrid. Special attention should be drawn to the original engraving of the map of Madrid, sketched by Pedro Teixeira in 1654 and the scale model of old Madrid constructed by León del Palacio in 1833. This model features all of the existing streets of

Madrid of that period, represented house by house and copying faithfully the facade of each one of the structures, fountains and town monuments. A careful study of this model —which is naturally huge— will help us to grow familiar with the city. Even the slopes of the streets are perfectly reproduced in scale. This very unusual and uncommon object has an extraordinary documentary value.

of the painting «Allegory of the Villa of Madrid», by Francisco de Goya, commissioned by the Town Council and surrounded by a long and unusual history. The City's Monstrance, on display here, and used in the Corpus Christi processions, was made by Madrilenian silversmith Francisco Alvarez in 1574 and is a work of great importance.

The Romantic Museum is located on nearby San Mateo Street and is a fine reproduction of what a well-to-do Madrid home would have looked like during the Romantic period. Paintings, furnishings, musical instruments, decorations, all of which combine to create an atmosphere of special charm and

↘ Army Museum.
⬆ Archaeological Museum.
⬅ Arab Room of the Army Museum.

↑ Municipal Museum.

← □ One aspect of the facade of the Municipal Museum.

← Fountain of Fame.

Cervantes street, takes us into a magical world. It was the home where the famous poet and playwright lived and died and it is furnished in part with many of his personal pieces of furniture and objects and complemented with other items belonging to the period. We can appreciate here how the middle-class Madrilenian lived in the 17th century.

The *Cerralbo Museum,* on Calle

modern and historical dating. Among the fascinating variety of valuable items on display is the unique collection of *Nacimientos* or Nativity Scenes made from every kind of material and proceeding from every epoch and just about every country.

We should also make mention of the *Bullfight Museum* located in the Las Ventas bullring itself and containing objects of different

periods of historic and emotional value as well as stuffed bull's heads which were conserved because of their bravery or, perhaps, their tragic historical significance.

Under this chapter, we should not neglect to cite museums which we have already covered more extensively in other sections of the book such as the Royal Palace, the Descalzas Reales and the Monastery of the Encarnación.

We also wish to include here a brief visit to the *Museum of the Royal Academy of History* (Calle León), which has some truly important pre-historic objects such as the Campanulate vessels from Ciempozuelos, the silver plate of Teodosius, an excellent piece of

historical significance.

The Museum of Modern Art, at the University City, has a highly valuable collection, despite its limited historical span. The work of contemporary painters and sculptors on display in the Museum have been carefully selected to help the visitor appreciate the present artistic movements going on in Spain, in its correct perspective.

The *House of Lope de Vega,* on

Ferraz, is another private foundation which was the Palace-Home of the Marquis of Cerralbo. The Marquis' extensive collection of art work, paintings, weapons and representative objects of different periods are exhibited here; there are some pieces of capital importance.

A visit to the *Museum of Decorative Arts,* at Calle Montalbán, can prove particularly interesting for it covers different themes of both

◿ Royal Tapistry Factory.

⬆ Fabrics.

◿ Open-air Museum of Modern Art. Paseo de la Castellana.

⬆ Museum of Contemporany Art.
⬅ Gardens of the Museum.

Roman art, engravings, drawings, paintings and thousands of manuscripts.

Also to be included in our list is the *Royal Tapistry Factory,* which continues to carry out its mission in accordance with old craft methods, producing magnificent hand-woven pieces, which reproduce the work of Spain's greatest painters.

Founded during the second half of the 18th century, the *Museum of America* exhibits archaeological objects discovered on the American continents, during the period when they were under Spanish control, as well as other items which were collected on scientific expeditions, expressly organized in the 18th century.

The *Ethnological Museum* at the end of Calle Alfonso XII, had its origins in the collection amassed by Dr. González Velasco, the famous 19th century surgeon. Here we can

find drawings, skeletons and sculptural reproductions of individuals who stand out because of their unusual physical appearance: giants, prognathics, dwarfs, etc., as well as paintings illustrating the results of inter-racial marriages. This Museum has articles dating from the Paleolithic period until the very present.

Upon the death of the Count and Countess of Valencia, their valuable

collection of art and historic objects made up the Foundation and *Museum of the Count, Don Juan de Valencia,* which was located in their Palace at Calle Fortuny, 43. Another building was put up in the garden area beside the original palace, in order to expand the quarters of the Foundations and an important library was incorporated into the Museum, which covered the most varied themes. We can make mention of the fabric collection, the best to be found in any of the Spanish museums, with pieces dating back to the 14th century as well as a beautiful red mantle of Nazarite Granada and the magnificent 16th century Arab rug with different inlaid colors and kid trimmings.

There are many interesting paintings including the *Alegoría de los Camaldulenses* by El Greco, from his last, masterful period, which represents the Virgin's protection to the friars of this religious order.

The House of Alba has collected the most important titles of Castile and England and as a result of marriages and successions, the Duchess of Alba holds approximately fifty aristocratic titles. The home of the Duke and Duchess is the *Palace of Liria,* on Calle Princesa, where they live surrounded by an extraordinary collection of art work dating back for centuries. The

18th century Palace was constructed by the Duke of Liria —this title is one of the many which eventually joined the long list accompanying that of the Dukedom of Alba.

As the Palace of Liria is the actual residence of the Duke and Duchess of Alba it can only visited with special permission.

Joaquín Sorolla y Bastida, the magical painter of shining light, was born in Valencia but he spent most of his life in Madrid until his death in 1923. The Museum dedicated to this great painter was installed in the mansion where he lived and had his studio. The museum contains not only a vast grouping of the painter's own works —though many of Sorolla's paintings are on display in museums throughout Europe and South America— but also those of contemporary painters which he had purchased in his lifetime.

The *Naval Museum* is certainly a specialized institution which will nevertheless prove interesting to the land-loving tourist. With a central location, near Cibeles Square, the Museum's collection was initiated with objects originally on display in Marine Headquarters and offices located throughout the peninsula and in South America.

Separate mention should be made of the museums of the Royal Patrimony: those contained in the Royal Palace and those found in the Convents of the Descalzas and the Encarnación, which should not be missed.

◥ One aspect of the Casón del Buen Retiro Museum.

◥ The Bullfight Museum.

↑   The Bullring. An aerial view.

←□ One aspect of a Bullring.

←   Statue to the Bullfighters.

Modern Madrid

Madrid has doubled in size over the past forty years and it has undergone so many transformations that some of its old quarters have taken on a new appearance. It is true that many of the newly constructed suburban areas are not worthy of any artistic admiration whatsoever; some are true urban aberrations but we feel that reference should be made to some of the more recent sections of this

Madrid of ours.

Perhaps one of the most visibly transformed areas is the Castellana, beginning at the Plaza de Colón. The first building which once stood on the right hand side of the street was a romantic mansion which should have been saved from demolition. Nothing was gained from its total destruction, for no other structure has as yet been put on the empty lot.

The Paseo de la Castellana is a very broad avenue which originally extended until the Plaza of San Juan de la Cruz. It was lined on either side with relatively modern palaces, born from the economic ecclosion produced by the restauration of the Monarchy in the person of Alfonso II, son of deposed Queen Isabel II, during the last quarter of the productive and affluent 19th century.

Today, the vast majority of aristocratic mansions are disappearing, pushed aside by new ways of life and strangled by property speculation. An example can be found in the old palace of Antonio Cánovas del Castillo, President of the Council of Ministers and a major influence in the Alfonsine restoration. This mansion stood on Serrano Street at the corner of today's Hermanos Bécquer street and its spacious garden and the so-called Huerta de Cánovas reached the Castellana. Tall buildings and two or three embassies now stand on the spot which was once occupied by the Palace, gardens and important library of the famous politician and

⬆ Gardens of the Discovery.

◤ Paseo de la Castellana. Monument to Castelar.

➡ New buildings on the Paseo de la Castellana.

↑ Colón Square and the Gardens of the Discovery.

← ▢ The City University.

↔ The Madrid «Metro».

historian. The old *Hipódromo* Ractrack, constructed in the afore-mentioned period, near the Plaza de San Juan de la Cruz, marked the end of the Paseo de la Castellana. The Racetrack has also disappeared but the thoroughfare was not extended until after the Spanish Civil War, when it was rapidly prolonged all the way to the Plaza de Castilla. In the center of this plaza is a monument to Calvo

Sotelo.

Construction on the University City was begun under the reign of King Alfonso XIII, but it was completely destroyed during the afore-mentioned Civil War. Its subsequent reconstruction required the addition of new buildings in order to carry out its full university functions. Today, the University is a beautiful complex in which the schools and faculties are interspersed throughout the attractive garden area.

The city's underground system, known as the «Metro» for short, is one of the indispensable means of transportation in this big city, which is forever growing.

When the old train stations of Norte and Atocha or Mediodía became too small to handle all the railway traffic, a new central station, Estación de Chamartín, was built in the North of Madrid.

Torrespaña is the result of Spanish Television's need to expand their installations in order to cover their vast broadcasting requirements.

Other architectural complexes have gone up throughout the *Villa* occupying once fertile farmland and the empty lots left by demolished mansions. The former case applies to the building know as *Torres Blancas* (White Towers) erected at the beginning of the Barajas

motorway, whose original and unique design has earned it major critical acclaim.

And finally, reference should be made to the major soccer stadiums in Madrid, that of the *Real Madrid* team on the Castellana and that of the *Atlético* team on the shores of the Manzanares. Though there are other stadiums in Madrid, they cannot match the mammoth size of these two popular *estadios*.

There is also an important auto racing circuit which was recently constructed at Jarama, near Madrid, for the celebration of major racing competitions.

◥ Soccer Stadium of the Club Atlético de Madrid.
◄ Jarama racetrack.
▣ MADRID 2. Shopping Center.

⬆ ACZA Area.

⬅☐ Real Madrid Soccer Stadium.

⬅ A building on the Paseo de la Castellana.

↑ Paseo de la Castellana.

☐ ➡ Chamartín Station.

➡ Torrespaña. TV Tower.

↓ Torres Blancas building.

The «Rastro» flea market

On the site where the city's slaughterhouses and tanneries were located —to which the street *Ribera de Curtidores* owes its name— the open-air market of the *Rastro* is set up on Sundays and holidays and it has achievied international fame.

The history of this market is indeed unusual. In the 15th century, King Juan II of Castile suddenly decided to take away Madrid's seigniory over the towns of Griñón

and Cubas, on behalf of one of his own protegés, Luis de la Cerda. He compensated Madrid by granting the city the right to hold two annual fairs. The *Ferias*, open-air markets where purchases and sales were not subject to any tax or duty of any kind, represented in the Middle Ages a great source of wealth and prosperity to the different Castilian communities. These fairs were held on St. Michael's Day and St.

Matthew's. In time, both of these fairs were combined on St. Matthew's Day at the end of September, which was more in keeping with the needs of the agricultural economy which existed at the time.

Time eventually diminished the importance of this old concession and the fairs slowly degenerated into simple markets for old pieces of furniture and junk which were set

up in diverse corners of the City. The *Rastro* finally settled itself on Ribera de Curtidores Street.

There was a time when some truly extraordinary discoveries could be made in the Rastro. Sometimes, highly valuable paintings, images or furniture were confused among relatively worthless material and were sold by the unaware vendors for a slight profit over the price they had originally paid. This is no longer the case.

At the beginning of the main avenue of Ribera de Curtidores, is a statue to Eloy Gonzalo. This Madrid hero, raised in the Town Orphanage, was a symbol of courage and heroism during the Cuban War of 1898.

↑ Municipal District Board.
↘ Ribera de Curtidores street.
↩ Monument to Eloy Gonzalo.

74

Casa de Campo, the Zoo and the Amusement Park

In the 16th century and once Madrid was established as the capital of Spain, Felipe II purchased a huge plot of land from one of the most important Madrid families, the Vargases. The property was located near the Palace —it was still an old Arab Alcázar (fortress)— but on the other side of the river. Today it is known as the Casa de Campo.

Thus, the Casa de Campo was initially intended for the pleasure and enjoyment of Kings and for centuries it was used mostly for hunting. As Madrid grew in size, it became necessary to turn this property over to the City.

A lake located on the terrain enhances its popular attraction and gives Madrilenians the opportunity to go row-boating or fishing.

The Madrid Zoo and the Amusement Park are also located within this broad extensión of natural land. Both installations can be reached from the city center by roads and bus lines, as well as a funicular which leaves from the Parque del Oeste and takes the visitor, suspended from high cables, across the river, the Paseo de la Florida, and the Sanctuary of San Antonio with its famous Goya frescos.

The modern Madrid Zoo has a magnificent arrangement in which the animals are kept in relative

freedom and in areas which try to recreate as much as possible the animal's natural habitat.

The Amusement Park has a fine collection of rides and attractions, together with several bars, restaurants and a large outdoor auditorium.

◤ Monument to Félix Rodríguez de la Fuente.
↑ A view of the Casa de Campo lake.
▸□ The Rosales-Casa de Campo funicular.
▸ The Panda in the Madrid Zoo.

↑ The Amusement Park. An aerial view.

←☐ The Amusement Park.

←☐ The Zoo.

77

The province, the outskirts of Madrid, the Pardo.

We have already made brief mention of El Pardo when we spoke about the iron gate of Puerta del Hierro. Initially a royal property, it has been a favorite hunting spot since the Middle Ages. Enrique IV, the King with an interesting yet unfortunate history, spent long periods of time, here, as did his successors, especially since Alfonso XI. Carlos I had his original house demolished and constructed a

new palace here which was expanded by Carlos III. Alfonso XII died in this Palace which years later would become the official residence of Chief of State General Francisco Franco. Today, the Pardo Palace is used to accomodate visiting Chiefs of State.

Another royal possession, the Moncloa Palace, is located near the Parque del Oeste and the University City which we have already

discussed.

The Palace of the Zarzuela is located within the Casa de Campo limits. Construction was begun on the palace in the year 1625 when it was considered little more than a hunting pavilion. It was first used by Prince Fernando, son of Felipe III, the Cardinal of Royal birth, who led an exemplary military life in Catalonia, Milan and especially in the Netherlands, during the Thirty Year War.

It was here during the 17th centuring that the first performances of a new theatrical form were put on: The *Zarzuela*. The first zarzuela, a kind of operetta which took its name from the Palace, was written by Calderón de la Barca with the title of «The Laurel Wreath of Apollo».

Today, the Palace of the Zarzuela, which has been subject to repeated renovation and expansion on several occasions over the centuries, is the official residence of the Spanish Royal Family. Juan Carlos I, as Prince of Spain, married Sophia of Schleswig-Holstein, daughter of King Pablo I and Frederica of Greece on May 14th, 1962.

⬆ El Pardo Palace.
◤ El Pardo Palace. One of the rooms.
◤ El Pardo Palace. The library.

⬆ Interior patio of the El Pardo Palace.

⬌▢ Gardens of the El Pardo Palace.

⬌ A room of the Palace.

Alcalá de Henares

Alcalá de Henares makes its historical appearance during the times of the Roman Empire with the name of Complutum. Enlarged by the Emperior Trajan, it kept its name and importance during the Gothic domination; it was called Guad-Alcalá or Al-kala-Nahar by the Arabs because of its river, which is the Henares. It was reconquered by the Archbishop of Toledo between 1088 and 1188, who would conserve

control and seigniory over the place for several centuries. The Courts drew up the famous «Ordinance of Alcalá» here in 1348. Cardinal Cisneros founded the famous University in this City; it was the forerunner of Madrid's higher educational institution, which is also called the Complutense, in honor of Alcalá de Henares. The same Cardinal had the Complutense Polyglot Bible printed here, a

magnum work of the Renaissance period. The University was moved to Madrid in 1836 but just recently a new University has been created within the old college quarters.

Alcalá de Henares is indeed an old city of great background and ancestry and it had a great deal of cultural and artistic importance for centuries.

It would be useless to attempt to offer a guide to Alcalá here for we

would need at least an entire book like this one to do the city justice. The old quarter deserves an unrushed visit, especially, of the numerous buildings which are distributed throughout the University area, the soul for centuries, along with Salamanca's University, of Spanish culture. Alcalá still conserves many important churches and monasteries, though a great number have been destroyed.

Alcala's old streets are still filled with a nostalgic University ambience, and many of the students who studied here went on to form part of Spain's most glorious history and literature. We should not forget that it was the birthplace of Miguel de Cervantes Saavedra.

→ Cervantes House.
↗ Monument to Cervantes.
↓ The ramparts.

↑ Facade of the University.

⊞ ☐ A square.

⊞ Facade of the Church. Gothic.

Aranjuez

Felipe II purchased the Aranjuez property from the Order of Santiago with the intention of building a town dedicated exclusively to the rest and relaxations of Kings. Anyone not a member of the Royal House was prohibited from establishing residence here until the 18th century when Fernando VI ordered a new town to be built.

Felipe II began construction on the Palace which was alternately continued and abandoned by his successors until Carlos III decided to complete the Residence. As a result, the decoration and gardens of the Royal Town of Aranjuez have a marked 18th century air.

If a visit to the Palace, its outbuildings, decorations and treasured furnishings prove interesting even more pleasurable will be a tour of the gardens which took on special importance during the reigns of Fernando VI and

Carlos III, as well as the monarchs following Fernando VII.

The long curve carved out by the river as it passes by Aranjuez forms a part of the gardens. Fernando VI had his famous concerts performed here. The musicians played aboard one large boat while the King and his Court lounged on another. A museum in Aranjuez exhibits the richly carved, royal launches, which give us an idea of how the sad King

tried to elude his intimate problems.

Carlos IV had the *Casita del Labrador* (Farmer's Cottage) built and it is a typical example of the many small structures built in 18th century Europe and intended for the intimate relaxation of the Kings and princes during their country outings. These graceful little structures which cannot quite be considered mansions but which were lavishly decorated and funished were the typical whim of an ostentious and refined epoch.

The Palace, begun by Juan de Herrera and Juan de Toledo, conserves little of its original appearance as a result of fires and subsequent reconstructions.

↑ Gardens of the Palace. Apollo fountain.

↘ A corner of the Gardens.

← Entrance to the Prince's gardens.

→ An aerial view of the Palace.

Chinchón

Chinchón extends along the crest and slope of a hill which dominates a fertile valley in the province of Madrid.

Chinchón possesses an interesting parish church, several sanctuaries, two convents, a few other institutions and two castles which were founded by Andrés Cabrera and the Count of Puñonrrostro, respectively. However, the true merit and charm of the town lies in the

fact that it has know how to conserve its traditional urban architecture and ambience intact, without submitting the town's homes and buildings to any major change. The main square is a magnificent example of what old rural *plazas mayores* of the towns of Castilla were like.

This main square as every *plaza mayor*, including Madrid's (which set out the lines for all the main squares in the rest of Spain and America) was the stage for the celebration of all the major fiestas of the community. Even today, bullfights are held in Chinchón on its typical feast days and wooden barriers and old carriages are used to enclose the temporary arena while the dissimilar but at the same time beautiful arcades and balconies of the square overflow with spectators.

In addition, the fact that, at one time, the priest of the local church was a brother of Francisco de Goya explains why the great artist painted a huge canvas for the main altar. This fine work can fortunately still be admired today. This is Chinchón's other glory.

Chinchón has been manufacturing its very famous anisette for centuries and now it is gaining international prestige. With a high alcoholic content but a delicate flavor, Chinchon's anisette has become a very popular drink.

↑ The square of Chinchón.
↖ A typical corner.
← The National Parador of Chinchón.
← The Manzanares el Real Castle.

The Guadarrama Range, Navacerrada, Cercedilla, El Escorial and the Valley of the Fallen

huge Valley of the Fallen, defying the strong sierra winds. A Church, crypt and place of study was built in the Cuelgamuros Valley and was intended to receive the remains of the soldiers fallen on both sides, during the Spanish Civil War. A great stone cross, of colossal dimensions, rises above the Basilica excavated from within the very mountain itself. At the foot of the Cross are the gigantic statues

Felipe II chose a place in the mountains for the grandiose monastery which was to be located precisely on the site of an old slag heap, hence its name: «El Escorial». Dedicated to the victory of the Spanish solders at the Battle of San Quintín, the Monastery of El Escorial was considered to be the Eighth Wonder of the World.

Part church, part Monastery, part Pantheon and part Royal Residence,

it doubled as a place of meditation and study. The grandiose but well proportioned building was furnished with royal generosity by its founder: books, manuscripts, relics, images, paintings, gold and silver work, ornaments, everything was provided in great abundance, making the whole a unique and unmatched structure.

Of modern constructión and located near El Escorial stands the

representing the four Evangelists, the work of Juan de Avalos, as well as the Pietá, also of huge dimensions which stands above the doorway of the Basilica. The architect, who directed this unique work of formidable proportions, was Diego Méndez.

◥ The El Escorial Monastery. The Library.
↑ Peñalara lake.
◥ Rascafría.
↔ Navácerrada Peak.

⬆ The El Escorial Monastery.

⬅☐ The Valley of the Fallen.

⬅ Inside the Basilica of the Valley of the Fallen.

➡ The El Escorial Monastery. An aerial view.

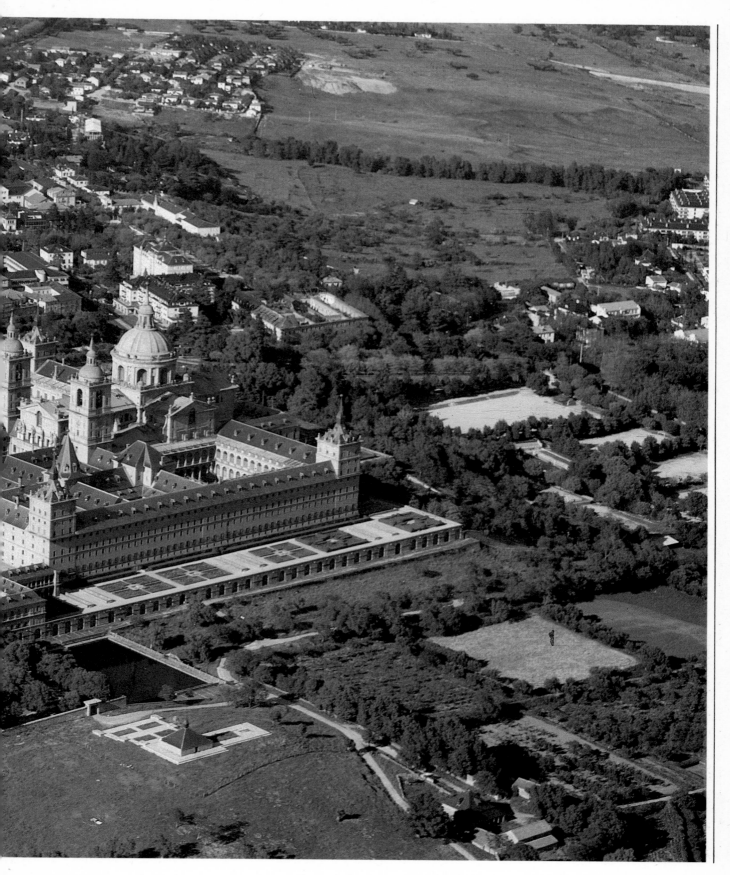

Excursions to the Guadarrama sierra and Segovia

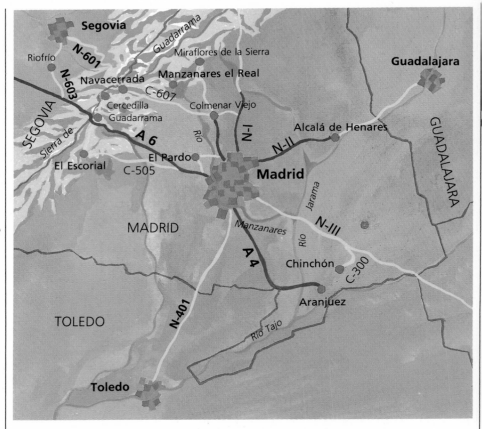

It was only in this century that the Madrilenians dared to approach the nearby mountain range with any great frequency. Up until then its difficult access was braved only by travellers heading to the Spanish capital from the North.

However, once the sierra was discovered, interest grew year after year. The Puerto de Cotos peak, at the foot of Cabeza de Hierra, with the nearby Peñalara lake, and its dark cold waters, is a fine starting point for excursions and for the preparation of more difficult climbs. Navacerrada is a great place for skiing and farther on are La Maliciosa and Montón de Trigo. On the other side of the mountain range, the northern slope offers the beautiful and rugged access of the Siete Revueltas (Seven Curves).

The nearby Madrid sierra is a magnificent place for summer vacationing, far away from the

rigors of a pressing heat. For the past few years, urban developments and private homes have sprouted up throughout the area giving it a bright and pleasant physiognomy.

Segovia is an old city with an ancient history. The Romans were so fond of this settlement that they wanted to quench the thirst of their farmlands by building the famous Aqueduct which still stands proud and intact today. The highest point of the Aqueduct is found at the Plaza del Azoguejo, which Cervantes dubbed the «Landmark and Cathedral of Picaresque life».

Segovia is a monumental city, filled with old mansions and convents and churches of different styles, presenting the city as a complete treatise on the History of Art. Its late and beautiful Cathedral and its Alcázar, renovated and recomposed a hundred times over, crown the city with a lovely and suggestive profile. Segovia's surroundings include a series of very interesting places of interest including the Palace and Gardens of La Granja and Valsaín, with its winding river —the Boca del Asno— and the huge pine groves which enclose the old wooden houses of the town.

◩ Segovia. La Granja.

◩ The Navacerrada Peak.

↑ The Alcázar of Segovia.
⇄□ The Aqueduct of Segovia.
⇄ The Cathedral of Segovia.

Toledo

Toledo is a real museum-city which must be included among the most important in Europe. In Toledo, the Imperial City, the best of three major cultures is conserved. The Arabs, who made it the capital of one of their peninsular kingdoms, the Jews who lived here and made it one of the most prosperous communities in their history and the Christians who made it the head of the important Archidiocese in Spain.

Toledo is filled with history and legends, lovingly woven together over the centuries. We can say that on a visit to Toledo's winding, narrow streets and squares, in the shadow of ancient temples, we will not find a single stone or a single piece of iron, which has not seen the passage of significant chapters of our History.

Its Cathedral was once the headquarters of a body which was,

for centuries, more influential than the Spanish kings themselves. As a result, the structure is a magnificent combination of art and wealth conserving the most outstanding elements of every century.

From a faraway land, the eastern island of Crete, at the other end of the Mediterranean, an unusual painter came to Toledo, never to leave the city. He lived between its walls, created his incomparable art

and died. His name was Domenico Theotocopuli, better known as El Greco.

And as a city of noble lineage, Toledo still possesses and practices a good deal of the rich craftwork which was inherited in part from its Arab ancestors. Toledo is famous for the **damasquinado** gold inlaid work, in which the artisan patiently hammers gold leaf into steel to create beautiful decorative adornments. We should not neglect to mention the swords of Toledo, of tempered steel, which were famous in their day, and which are still considered unique in the whole world. These blades are manufactured in the same way today as they were made centuries ago.

⬆ Toledo. A scenic view.

↘ The ramparts.

⬆ The Cathedral of Toledo.

⬅☐ The inside of the Cathedral.

⬅ One aspect of the facade of the Cathedral.

Guadalajara and the outskirts of Madrid

Since 1561, when Madrid was chosen by Felipe II as the center and seat of his kingdom, Madrid's surroundings have undergone a striking transformation.

There were many factors which influenced the unfortunate results. The first was perhaps the need for wood to attend to the ever increasing demand for the construction of new homes. It was also necessary to plough up more

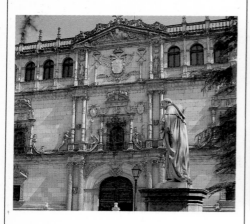

and more of the fields in order to obtain produce with which to feed the hungry city. The draughts which are so customary in this part of Spain must also have been a contributing factor in the conversion of much of the area into barren land.

In the 17th century, foreigners arriving to Madrid must have been surprised at the sudden appearance of this big city in the middle of the steppe of the lower Castilian plateau.

Today, with the exception of Aranjuez, which appears as an oasis to the traveller and the nearby mountains, the Madrid countryside, wheatland for the most part, has been ceding its space to the constant construction and expansion of the city. And if Madrid grew and grew over the years, the time soon came for the encircling towns to spread out until they too took over the fields where wheat, peppers and tomatoes had grown.

Standing out on the vast flat plain of the Cerro de los Angeles, is an isolated hill rising up close to the city, which is considered the geographic center of Spain. A Sanctuary was erected on this site dedicated to the Heart of Jesus and the figure of the Redeemer can be seen from great distances.

In the opposite direction, past Alcalá de Henares, of which we have already spoken, is Guadalajara, a once wealthy community, which underwent a major period of decadence. Once again today it is taking on new importance and activity.

⬆ The Cerro de los Angeles hill.
⬅ The Alcalá de Henares University.
⬉ The Archbishop's Palace of Alcalá de Henares.

On Madrid Cooking

Madrid represents the unchallenged core of Spanish cuisine for within its municipal limits, we can find places which offer all of the popular dishes of the country's regional cooking. However, together with this luxury of out-of-town cooking, Madrid also has its own cuisine, a cuisine which is laced with contributions from La Mancha. It is also a cuisine which was shaped in the 16th century when Felipe II converted the *Villa y Corte de Madrid* into the capital of Spain, thus attracting the top French, Flemish and especially Italian chefs to the city.

We can say that Madrid'gastronomical literature began with the *Libro del Arte de Cocina* (The Book on the Art of Cooking), written by Diego Granado, reflecting an overwhelming Italian influence. It was published in Madrid in 1599 and was followed by the *Arte de Cocina,* by Francisco Martínez Montiño, the royal chef. This book offers a perfect panorama of how the Court of Felipe III feasted on internationalized cooking, without excluding some truly traditional Spanish dishes.

As an example of the typical *figones* or eating establishments, existing in that period, we can suggest the classic restaurant of Botín, which has managed to survive over the years. Located in the Plaza de Herradores since 1620, the date of its foundation, this restaurant was famous for its puff pastry and above all, for its roast lamb and pig. In addition to this tavern *(mesón),* there were others which were famous for their fine cooking and which were immortalized by the writers of the Golden Century, among which we can mention the Mesón de Paredes,

previously called «La Fama», La Posada del Dragón, which took its name from the famous serpent of Puerta Cerrada, the León de Oro, the Restaurant de la Villa, that of El Segoviano, and many others including some which were harshly mistreated by the French in their literature.

In truth prior to the end of the 19th century, The Villa was not distinguished for the quality of its restaurants and boarding houses. Nevertheless, some famous names have reached us, such as La Fontana de Oro, which was located in 1760 in the Carrera de San Jerónimo and was a den of conspirators and extremists, who played active roles in the tumultous politics of the period. The Fonda de San Sebastián was founded by the Gippini brothers in the Calle de Atocha in around 1767 and was the site for Nicolás Fernández de Moratín's *tertulia* or literary coterie.

Contemporary to this establishment was the Fonda de Genieys, located in the Calle Reina, a meeting place for many of the romantic writers of the day and the home of composer Joaquín Rossini, who was a noted

gourmet.

At the end of the 19th century, the taste of the Madrilenians grew more refined, surely due to the influences received from abroad. Some truly fine restaurants were opened in Madrid which were able to match the quality of those abroad. In this category, we can mention «Tournié», in the Calle Mayor, with a very unusual and refined cuisine, offered, at the time, at high prices. At a lesser level, we can cite Los Burgaleses, on Calle Príncipe. However, if we wanted to

eat well but at more reasonable prices, there was La Viña P, also in Calle Príncipe, with an ample variety of fish and seafood. Stiff competition was offered by L'Hardy, on the Carrera de San Jerónimo, a meeting place for the most influential people in the city, and a bit of its past fame still lingers on today. The restaurant Fornos, at Calle Alcalá on the corner of Peligros street, was frequented by intellectuals, politicians and the most famous folk, and its private dining rooms were the setting for many episodes in the very active Spanish social life of the time. Petit Fornos, on Calle Capellanes, should be mentioned, a cenacle for bohemians and noctambulists. We could go on naming the important historic restaurants of our city but the list would prove endless.

In contemporary times, Spanish life has changed considerably and one can dine at some truly fine restaurants throughout the city which can bear comparison with the most famous establishments abroad. I prefer to leave more detailed mention of the contemporary restaurants to another pen which is in a better position to contemplate the present panorama with a greater perspective.

José Luis

Useful addresses and Telephone Numbers

Town Council: Information, Plaza de la Villa, 5. Tel. 248 10 00.
Plaza Mayor, 27. Tel. 266 66 00.
Municipal Police Headquarters: Emergencies. Tel. 092.
Police, General Body: Emergencies. Tel. 0,91.
Delegations of the Autonomic Government: Mayor, 69. Tel. 479 30 11.
Autonomic Government.
Social Security: Emergencies. Tel. 734 55 00.
RENFE (Spanish Railways): Alcalá, 44. Information. Tels. 733 22 00 y 733 30 00.
Barajas Airport: Information. Tels. 205 43 72 and 231 44 36.
Fire Department. Tel. 232 32 32.
O.R.A.: Street Parking Control. Alberto Aguilera, 20. Tel. 447 17 09.
Telephone of Hope. Tel. 239 20 31.
Taxi Radio-Telephone. Tel. 247 82 00.
Radio-Taxi. Tel. 409 90 00.
Teletaxi. Tel. 445 90 08.
Red Cross Drug Assistance Center: Fuencarral, 8. Tel. 429 38 13.
Tele-Ruta (Information on Highway Conditions). Tel. 441 72 22.
Weather report. Tel. 094.
Condition of highways. Tel. 253 16 00 (ext. 2397).
O.R.A.: Alberto Aguilera, Tel. 447 07 13.
City and tourist information: Plaza de la Villa, 3. Tel. 266 66 00.
The Zoo: Casa de Campo. Tel. 711 99 50.
The Amusement Park: Casa de Campo. Tel. 463 29 00.
Dog racing track: Vía Carpetana, 57. Tel. 471 21 00.
La Zarzuela Horse-racing track: Carretera La Coruña, km. 7. Tel. 207 01 40.

Madrid Gambling Casino: Carretera La Coruña, km. 28,3. Tel. 859 03 12.
Information on religious worship in different languages. Tel. 241 48 04.

Travel Agencies

Viajes Conde: Princesa, 7. Tel. 247 18 04.
Av. Mediterráneo, 37. Tel. 251 41 38.
Club de Vacaciones: Goya, 23. Tel. 276 24 08.
Juliatours: Capitán Haya, 38. Tel. 270 43 00.
Pullmantur: Plaza Oriente, 8. Tel. 241 18 07.
Turavia: Vizconde de Matamala, 7. Tel. 246 30 00.
Turvisa: San Bernardo, 5-7. Tel. 241 92 10.
Trapsatur: San Bernardo, 23. Tel. 241 44 07.
Urituvi: Gran Vía, 55. Tel. 247 29 55.
American Express: Plaza Cortes, 2. Tel. 222 11 80.
Wagons Lits Cook: Alcalá, 23. Tel. 433 56 00.
Viajes El Corte Inglés: Preciados, 3. Tel. 221 38 58.
Marsans: Alberto Alcocer, 19. Tel. 458 11 50.
Viajes Meliá: Princesa, 25. Tel. 247 55 00.
Ecuador: Carrera de San Jerónimo, 19. Tel. 221 46 04.

Airlines

Iberia: Information. Cánovas del Castillo, 4. Tel. 411 25 45.
Aviaco: Maudes, 51. Tel. 234 46 00.
Spantax: Paseo de la Castella, 181. Tel. 279 69 00.
Lufthansa: Gran Vía, 88. Tel. 247 19 07.
Aerolíneas Argentinas: Princesa, 12. Tel. 247 47 00.
British Airways: Gran Vía, 68. Tel. 247 53 00.
Air France: Gran Vía, 55. Tel. 247 20 00.
KLM: Gran Vía, 59. Tel. 247 81 00.
Alitalia: Princesa, 1. Tel. 247 46 05
Kuwait Airwais: Princesa, 1. Tel. 242 03 17.
Aeroméxico: Princesa, 1. Tel. 247 99 00.
Varig: Gran Vía, 88. Tel. 248 62 04.
TWA: Gran Vía, 68. Tel. 247 42 00.
Aeroflot: Princesa, 25. Tel. 241 99 34.
Swissair: Gran Vía, 88. Tel. 247 92 07.
British-Airways: Gran Vía, 68. Tel. 248 78 06.
Sabena: Gran Vía, 88. Tel. 241 89 05.
SAS: Gran Vía, 88. Tel. 247 17 00.

Automobile Companies

Citröen: Doctor Esquerdo, 62. Tel. 274 78 00.
Renault: Avenida de Burgos, 89. Tel. 766 00 00.

Seat-Audi-BMW: Paseo de la Castellana, 278. Tel. 215 33 40.
Talbot, Peugeot: Carretera de Villaverde, km. 7,5. Tel. 797 26 00.
Fiat: Habana, 74. Tel. 747 11 11.
Mercedes Benz: Don Ramón de la Cruz, 105. Tel. 401 60 00.
Volvo: Paseo de la Castellana, 130. Tel. 262 22 07.
Ford: Paseo de la Castellana, 135. Tel. 279 95 00.

Auto Assistance

Real Automóvil Club, Race: Abascal, 10. Tel. 447 32 00.
ADA: A. Herrero, 9. Tel.: 450 10 00.
Europ Assistance: Orense, 2. Tel. 456 39 99.

Car Rental Agencies

Regent-Car: Avenida Reina Victoria, 13. Tel. 234 10 04.
Avis: Gran Vía, 60. Tel. 247 20 48.
Hertz: Edificio España, local 18. Tel. 242 10 00.
Europcar: Orense, 29. Tel. 455 99 31.
Estación Sur Autobuses: Canarias, s/n. Tel. 468 42 00.

Museums

Prado Museum: Paseo del Prado, s/n. Tels. 239 06 15 and 468 09 50.
Archaeological Museum: Serrano, 13. Tels. 403 65 59 and 403 66 07.
Museum of Contemporary Art: Juan de Herrera, 2. Tels. 449 71 50 and 449 24 53.

Museum of America: Avenida Reyes Católicos, 6. Tels. 449 24 53 and 449 26 41.
Velázquez Palace: Parque del Retiro.
Tels. 274 77 75 and 274 20 42.
National Museum of Ethnology: Alfonso XII, 68. Tel. 230 64 18.
Museum of Decorative Arts: Montalbán, 12. Tel. 221 34 40.
Lázaro Galdiano Museum: Serrano, 122. Tels. 261 60 84 and 261 49 79.
Naval Museum: Montalbán, 2. Tel. 221 04 19.
Museum of the Spanish People: Atocha, 106. Tel. 228 50 39.
Romantic Museum: San Mateo, 13. Tel. 448 10 71.
Sorolla Museum: General Martínez Campos, 37. Tel. 410 15 84.
Wax Museum: Plaza Colón. Tel. 419 22 82.

Cerralbo Museum: Ventura Rodríguez, 17. Tel. 247 36 46.
Army Museum: Méndez Núñez, 1. Tel. 222 06 28.
Municipal Museum: Fuencarral, 78. Tel. 221 66 56.
National Museum of Ethnology: Alfonso XII, 6. Tel. 239 59 95.
Casón del Buen Retiro: Felipe IV, 13. Tel. 230 91 14.
Annex to the Casón del Buen Retiro: Alfonso XII, 28. Tel. 230 91 14.
National Museum of Artistic Reproductions: Edificio M. Américas. Tel. 244 14 47.
Bullfight Museum: Plaza Monumental de las Ventas. Tel. 255 18 57.
Royal Palace: Bailén, s/n. Tel. 248 74 04.
Royal Academy of Fine Arts: Paseo Recoletos,

20. Tel. 276 25 64.
House of Alba Foundation: Princesa, 20. Tel. 247 66 06.
National Coin and Stamp Factory: Doctor Esquerdo, 36. Tel. 274 50 05.
Monastery of Descalzas Reales: Plaza Descalzas Reales, 3. Tel. 222 06 87.
Monastery of La Encarnación: Plaza Encarnación, 1. Tel. 247 05 10.
Bank of Spain: Alcalá, 50. Tel. 446 90 55.
Bishop's Chapel: Plaza Marqués de Comillas, s/n. Tel. 265 49 63.
Institute of Don Juan de Valencia: Fortuny, 43. Tel. 419 87 74.
Open-air Sculpture Museum: Paseo de la Castellana.
Benedito Collection: Juan Bravo, 4. Tel. 275 46 87.
El Pardo Palace: El Pardo. Tel. 222 28 65.

Theatres

Theatre Alcalá-Palace: Alcalá, 90. Tel. 435 46 08.
Theatre Bellas Artes: Marqués de Casa Riera, 2. Tel. 232 44 37.
Theatre Calderón: Atocha, 18. Tel. 239 13 33.
Centro Cultural Villa de Madrid: Plaza de Colón.
Theatre de la Comida: Príncipe, 14. Tel. 221 49 31.
Theatre Cómico: Paseo de las Delicias, 41. Tel. 227 45 37.
Theatre Espronceda-34: Espronceda, 34. Tel. 442 76 50.
Theatre Fígaro: Doctor Cortezo, 5. Tel. 239 16 45.
Theatre Fuencarral: Fuencarral, 133. Tel. 248 27 48.
Theatre Infanta Isabel: Barquillo, 24. Tel. 221 47 78.
Theatre La Latina: Plaza Cebada, 2. Tel. 265 28 35.
Theatre Lara: Corredera Baja de San Pablo, 15. Tel. 232 82 12.
Theatre Maravillas: M. Malasaña, 6. Tel. 447 41 35.
Theatre Martín: Santa Brígida, 3. Tel. 231 63 93.
Theatre Monumental: Atocha, 65. Tel. 227 12 14.
Theatre Muñoz Seca: Plaza del Carmen. Tel. 221 90 47.
Theatre Príncipe Gran Vía: Tres Cruces, 10. Tel. 221 80 16.
Theatre Reina Victoria: Carrera San Jerónimo, 22. Tel. 429 58 90.

Theatre del Círculo: Círculo Bellas Artes, Alcalá, 42. Tel. 231 33 37.
Theatre María Guerrero: Tamayo y Baus, 4. Tel. 419 47 69.
Theatre Español: Príncipe, 25. Tel. 429 62 97.
Sala Olimpia: Plaza de Lavapiés. Tel. 227 46 22.
Theatre de la Zarzuela: Jovellanos, 4. Tel. 429 82 16.

Restaurants with Shows

Florida Park: Parque del Retiro. Tels. 273 78 04 and 273 78 05.
La Terraza de Mayte: Plaza República Argentina, 5. Tel. 261 86 06.
Noches de Cuplé: Palma, 51. Tel. 232 71 75 and 232 71 16.

Rancho Criollo: Carretera de La Coruña, km. 17. Tel. 637 50 36 and 637 17 11.
Scala Meliá Castilla: Rosario Pino, 7. Tel. 450 44 00.

Restaurants

Al-Mounia: Recoletos, 5. Tel. 275 01 73. Moroccan cooking.
Alkalde: Jorge Juan, 10. Tel. 276 33 59. Basque and South American Cooking.
Asador Donostiarra: Pedro Villar, 14. Tel. 279 62 64. Traditional Basque cooking.
Ascot: Plaza de la Moraleja (Alcobendas). Tel. 650 13 53. Central European and international cooking.
Bajamar: Gran Vía, 78. Tel. 248 59 03. Fish and seafood.

Balthasar: Juan Ramón Jiménez, 8. Hotel Eurobuilding. Tel. 457 91 91. International cooking.
Balzac: Moreto, 7. Tel. 239 19 22. Interesting novelties.
Bellman: Hotel Suecia, Marqués de Casa Riera, 4. Tel. 231 69 00. Scandinavian cooking and smorgasbord.
Cabo Mayor: Juan Hurtado de Mendoza, 11. Tel. 250 87 76. Imaginative cooking.
Café de Oriente. Plaza de Oriente, 2. Tel. 241 15 74. Luxury cuisine.
Clara's: Arrieta, 2. Tel. 242 00 71. French and Portuguese cooking.
Club 31: Alcalá, 58. Tel. 231 00 92. Classic cooking.
Colony: Alberto Alcocer, 43. Tel. 250 64 99. French-Libanese cooking.
Combarro: Reina Mercedes, 12. Tel. 254 77 84. Fish and seafood.
De Funy: Víctor Andrés Belaúnde, 1. Tel. 259 72 25. Libanese cooking.
El Amparo: Callejón de Puigcerdá, 8. Tel. 431 64 56. New, refined cooking.
El Bodegón: Pinar, 15. Tel. 262 31 37. Fine, classic cuisine.
El Circo: Ortega y Gasset, 29. Tel. 276 01 44. Modern cooking.
El Cosaco: Alfonso VI, 4. Tel. 265 35 48. Russian cuisine.
El Espejo: P.º de Recoletos, 31. Tel. 410 25 25. Traditional cuisine.
El Faisán de Oro: Bolivia, 11. Tel. 259 30 76. Imaginative cuisine.
El Gran Chambelán: Ayala, 46. Tel. 431 77 45. Top cuisine.
El Landó: Plaza de Gabriel Miró, 8. Tel. 266 76 81. Typical cuisine.
El Pescador: Ortega y Gasset, 75. Tel. 401 30 26. Fish and seafood.
Edelweiss: Jovellanos, 7. Tel. 221 03 26. German and Spanish cooking.
El Escuadrón: Tamayo y Baus, 8. Tel. 419 28 30. Top traditional cooking.
Gaztelupe: Comandante Zorita, 37. Tel. 253 51 52. Luxury Basque cooking.
Guria: Huertas, 12. Tel. 239 16 36. Classic Basque cooking.
Gure-Etxea: Plaza de la Paja, 12. Tel. 265 61 49. Traditional Basque cooking.
Horcher: Alfonso XII, 6. Tel. 222 07 31 y 232 35 96. Central European cooking.
Horno de Santa Teresa: Sta. Teresa, 12. Tel. 419 02 45. Traditional cooking.
Hotel Ritz: Plaza de la Lealtad, 5. Tel. 221 28 57. Aristocratic, luxury cooking.
Irizar-Jatetxea: Jovellanos, 3. Tel. 231 45 69.

Modern Basque cooking.
Itxaso: Capitán Haya, 58. Tel. 450 64 12. Luxury Basque cooking.
Jockey: Amador de los Ríos, 6. Tel. 419 10 03. Top, classic cuisine.
José Luis: Rafael Salgado, 17. Tel. 250 41 98. Traditional and Basque cooking.
L'Alsace: Domenico Scarlatti, 5. Tel. 244 40 75. Alsatian cuisine.
La Almoraima: Hotel Los Galgos, Diego de León, 3. Tel. 262 66 00. International cuisine.
La Dorada: Orense, 64-66. Tel. 270 20 04. Fish and Andalusian dishes.
La Fonda: Lagasca, 11, y Príncipe de Vergara, 211. Tel. 403 83 01 and 250 61 47. Top Catalonian cuisine.
La Fuencisla: San Mateo, 4. Tel. 221 61 86. Traditional Spanish cooking.
La Gabarra: Santo Domingo de Silos, 6. New luxury cooking.
La Máquina: Sor Angela de la Cruz, 22. Tel. 270 61 05. Luxury Asturian cooking.
La Marmite: Plaza de San Amaro, 8. Tel. 279 92 61. Classic French cooking.
La Trainera: Lagasca, 60. Tel. 435 89 54. Fish and seafood.
Las Cumbres: Alberto Alcocer, 32. Tel. 458 76 92. Andalusian fried dishes.
Las Cuatro Estaciones: General Ibáñez Ibero, 5. Tel. 253 63 05. Seasonal dishes.
Las Reses: Orfila, 3. Tel. 419 10 13. Meat.
Las Vigas: Prim, 15. Tel. 231 83 44. New dishes and desserts.
L'Hardy: Carrera de San Jerónimo, 8. Tel. 222 22 07. Open in 1839.
Los Remos: carretera Madrid-La Coruña. km. 12,700. Tel. 207 73 36. Fish and seafood.
Luarques: Ventura de la Vega, 16. Tel. 429 61 74. Magnificent quality/price relationship.
Mayte Commodore: Plaza República Argentina, 5. Tel. 261 86 06. Top Basque and international cuisine.
Mei-Ling: Paseo de la Castellana, 188. Tel. 457 67 17. Chinese cuisine.
Mikado: Pintor Juan Gris, 4. Tel. 456 30 43. Japanese cuisine.
Ordago: Sancho Dávila, 15. Tel. 246 71 85. Basque cuisine.
O'Pazo: Reina Mercedes, 20. Tel. 253 23 33. Fish and seafood.
Platerías: Plaza de Santa Ana, 11. Tel. 429 79 48. Pleasant cooking.
Portonovo: Carretera Madrid-La Coruña, km. 10,500. Tel. 207 07 52. Fish and seafood.
Príncipe de Viana: Manuel de Falla, 5. Tel. 259 14 48. Excellent Basque-Navarrese

cuisine.
Sacha: Juan Hurtado de Mendoza, 11. Tel. 457 59 52. Galician cuisine with specialties.
Saint James: Juan Bravo, 26. Tel. 275 00 69. Levantine rice dishes.
Sulu: P.ºCastellana, 172. Tel. 259 10 40. Philippine cooking.
Tattaglia: P.ºHabana, 17. Tel. 262 85 90. Italian cuisine.
Txistu: Plaza de Angel Carbajo. Tel. 270 96 51. Typical Basque cuisine.
Viridiana: Fundadores, 23. Tel. 246 90 40. Unusual cooking.
Zalacaín: Alvarez de Baena, 4. Tel. 261 48 40. Basque and international cuisine.

Near Madrid

In Aranjuez: El Castillo. Jardines del Príncipe. Tel. 891 30 00.
Casa Pablo. Hermano Guardiola, 20. Tel. 891 14 51.
In Alcalá de Henares: Hostería del Estudiante. Colegios, 3. Tel. 888 03 30.
In Boadilla del Monte: La Cañada. Carretera Boadilla, km. 8. Tel. 655 12 83.
In Fuencarral: El Mesón. Carretera Colmenar Viejo, km. 13,5. Tel. 734 10 19.
In Chinchón: Cuevas del Vino. Benito Hortelano, 13. Tel. 894 02 06.
Mesón de la Virreina. Plaza de Chinchón.
In El Pardo: Pedro's. Avenida de la Guardia. Tel. 736 08 83.
In San Lorenzo de El Escorial: Fonda Genara. Plaza de San Lorenzo, 2. Tel. 896 02 91.
In Pozuelo: Bodega la Salud. Jesús Gil

González. Tel. 715 33 90.
In Majadahonda: El Abolengo.
In Navacerrada: La Fonda Real. Carretera 601, km. 52. Tel. 856 03 05.
In Miraflores de la Sierra: Maíto. Calvo Sotelo, 5. Tel. 624 35 67.

Hotels

Ritz: Plaza de la Lealtad, 5. Tel. 221 28 57, 43986 ritze.
Palace: Plaza de las Cortes, 7. Tel. 429 75 51, 22272 ripal.
Villa Magna. Paseo de la Castellana, 22. Tel. 261 49 00, 22914 vima.
Alameda: Avenida Logroño, 100. Tel. 747 48 88, 43809 malae.
Barajas: Avenida Logroño, 305. Tel. 747 77 00,

22255 madas.
Eurobuilding: Padre Damián, 23. Tel. 457 17 00, 22548 eubil.
Luz Palacio: Paseo de la Castellana, 57. Tel. 442 51 00, 27207 luze.
Meliá Madrid: Princesa, 27. Tel. 241 82 00, 22537 metel.
Miguel Angel: Miguel Angel, 31. Tel. 442 81 99, 44235 homa.
Mindanao: San Francisco de Sales, 15. Tel. 449 55 00, 22631 minda.
Monte Real: Arroyo Fresno, 17. Tel. 216 21 40, 22089.
Princesa Plaza: Princesa, 40. Tel. 242 35 00, 44378 priz.
Wellington: Velázquez, 8. Tel. 275 44 00, 22700 velin.
Agumar: Paseo Reina Cristina, 7.

Tel. 252 69 00, 22814.
Aitana: Paseo de la Castellana, 152. Tel. 250 71 07, 49186 hait.
Alcalá: Alcalá, 66. Tel. 435 10 60, 48094.
Carlton: Paseo de las Delicias, 26. Tel. 239 71 00.
Castellana: Paseo de la Castellana, 49. Tel. 410 02 00, 27686.
Chamartín: Estación de Chamartín. Tel. 733 62 20, 49201 hchme.
Colón: Doctor Esquerdo, 117-119. Tel. 273 08 00, 22984 colo.
Convención: O'Donnell, 53. Tel. 274 68 00, 23944.
Cuzco: Paseo de la Castellana, 133. Tel. 456 06 00, 22464 cuzco.
Emperador: Gran Vía, 53. Tel. 247 28 00, 27521.
Escultor: Miguel Angel, 3. Tel. 410 42 03, 44285 haese.
Eurobuilding: Juan Ramón Jiménez, 8. Tel. 457 17 00, 22548.
Florida Norte: Paseo de la Florida, 5. Tel. 241 61 90, 23675.
Los Galgos: Claudio Coello, 139. Tel. 262 42 27, 43957 galge.
El Gran Atlanta: Comandante Zorita, 34. Tel. 253 59 00.
Gran Hotel Velázquez: Velázquez, 62. Tel. 275 28 00, 22779.
Meliá Castilla: Capitán Haya, 43. Tel. 270 84 00, 23142.
Pintor: Goya, 79. Tel. 435 75 45, 23281 asses.
Plaza: Plaza de España. Tel. 247 12 00, 27383.
Suecia: Marqués de Casa Riera, 4. Tel. 231 69 00, 22313.
Avión: Avenida de Aragón, 345.

Tel. 747 62 22.
Balboa: Núñez de Balboa, 112. Tel. 262 54 40.
Capitol: Gran Vía, 41. Tel. 221 83 91.
Centro Norte: Mauricio Ravel, 10. Tel. 733 34 00,42598.
Claridge: Plaza Conde de Casal, 6. Tel. 251 94 00.
Conde Duque: Plaza Conde Valle de Suchil, 5. Tel. 447 70 00, 22058 duque.
Cortezo: Doctor Cortezo, 3. Tel. 239 38 00.
Eurotel Madrid: Galeón, 27. Tel. 747 13 55, 45688 ermae.
Gran Vía: Gran Vía, 25. Tel. 222 11 21, 44173.
Praga: Antonio López, 65. Tel. 469 06 00, 22823.
Príncipe Pío: Cuesta de San Vicente, 14. Tel. 247 80 00, 42183 gabeo.
Puerta de Toledo: Glorieta Puerta de Toledo, 2. Tel. 474 71 00, 22291 hpeto.
Rex: Gran Vía, 43 duplicado. Tel. 247 48 00.
San Antonio de la Florida: Paseo de la Florida, 13. Tel. 247 14 00.
Tirol: Marqués de Urquijo, 4. Tel. 248 19 00.
Trafalgar: Trafalgar, 3. Tel. 445 62 00.
Victoria: Plaza del Angel, 7. Tel. 231 45 00.
Zurbano: Zurbano, 79 81. Tel. 441 55 00, 27578 otels.

Cafes

Comercial: Glorieta Bilbao, 7. Tel. 221 56 55.
Gijón: Paseo de Recoletos.
Lyon: Alcalá, 57. Tel. 275 00 51.
Manuela: San Vicente Ferrer, 29. Tel. 231 70 37.
Progreso: Cabeza, 5. Tel. 228 47 23.
Café de Ruiz: Ruiz, 14.
Tetería de la Abuela: Espíritu Santo, 19.

Embassies

Office of Diplomatic Information. Tel. 265 86 05.
Algeria: Zurbano, 100. Tel. 442 47 00.
Argentina: Paseo de la Castellana, 53. Tel. 442 45 00.
Austria: Paseo de la Castellana, 180. Tel. 250 92 00.
Belgium: Paseo de la Castellana, 18. Tel. 401 95 58.
Brazil: Fernando el Santo, 6. Tel. 419 12 00.
Canada: Núñez de Balboa, 35. Tel. 431 43 00.
Chile: Lagasca, 88. Tel. 431 91 60.
China: Arturo Soria, 111. Tel. 413 66 59.
Colombia: Martínez Campos, 48. Tel. 410 28 00.
Cuba: Paseo de la Habana, 194. Tel. 458 25 00.
Denmark: Claudio Coello, 91. Tel 433 30 00.
Dominican Republic: Paseo de la Castellana, 30. Tel. 431 53 21.
Egypt: Velázquez, 69. Tel 401 96 00.
Finland: Fortuny, 18. Tel. 419 22 62.
France: Salustiano Olózaga, 8. Tel. 433 55 60.
West Germany: Fortuny, 8. Tel. 457 12 50.
East Germany: Prieto Ureña, 6. Tel. 250 66 01.
Great Britain: Fernando el Santo, 16. Tel. 419 02 08.
Greece: Serrano, 110.Tel. 411 33 45.
Holland: Paseo de la Castellana, 64. Tel. 458 21 00.
India: Velázquez, 93. Tel. 413 61 61.
Iran: Jerez, 5. Tel. 457 01 12.
Iraq: Paseo de la Castellana, 83. Tel. 455 55 28.
Ireland: Hermanos Bécquer, 10. Tel. 413 56 12.
Italy: Lagasca, 98. Tel. 402 54 36.
Japan: Joaquín Costa, 29. Tel. 262 55 46.
Jordan: General Martínez Campos, 41. Tel. 419 11 00.
Kuwait: Paseo de la Castellana, 178. Tel. 458 87 18.
Lebanon: José Abascal, 47. Tel. 442 27 00.
Libya: Pisuerga, 12. Tel. 458 04 58.
Mauritania: Velázquez, 90. Tel. 275 07 07.
Mexico: Paseo de la Castellana, 93. Tel. 456 12 63.
Morocco: Serrano, 179. Tel. 548 80 18.
Netherlands: Paseo de la Castellana, 178. Tel. 458 21 00.
Norway: Juan Bravo, 3. Tel. 401 62 62.
Panama: Ortega y Gasset, 29. Tel. 401 84 00.

Paraguay: Castelló, 30. Tel. 435 88 58.
Peru: Príncipe de Vergara, 36. Tel. 431 42 42.
Philippines: Zurbano, 36. Tel. 419 59 58.
Portugal: Pinar, 1. Tel. 261 78 00.
Saudi Arabia: Paseo de La Habana, 163. Tel. 457 12 50.
South Africa: Claudio Coello, 91. Tel. 225 38 30.
Soviet Union: Maestro Ripoll, 14. Tel. 411 07 06.
Sweden: Zurbano, 27. Tel. 419 75 50.
Switzerland: Núñez de Balboa, 35. Tel. 431 34 00.
Thailand: Segre, 29. Tel. 250 38 72.
Tunisia: Plaza Alonso Martínez, 3. Tel. 447 35 08.
United Arab Emirates: Capitan Haya, 40. Tel. 270 10 04.
United States of America: Serrano, 75. Tel. 273 36 00.
Uruguay: Rosales, 32. Tel. 248 69 99.
Venezuela: Capitán Haya, 1. Tel. 455 84 53.

Discotheques

Bocaccio: M. Ensenada, 16. Tel. 419 10 08.
Green: Juan Bravo, 3. Tel. 276 77 69.
Joy Eslava: Arenal, 9. Tel. 266 54 39.
Long Play: Plaza Vázquez de Mella, 2. Tel. 231 01 11.
Mau-Mau: Juan Ramón Jiménez, 8. Tel. 250 27 57.
¡Oh!: Carretera de La Coruña, km. 6.
Pachá: Barceló, 11. Tel. 446 01 37.
Piña's: Alberto Alcocer, 33. Tel. 250 60 68.
Retro: Conde de Peñalver, 8. Tel. 435 67 38.
Rock-Ola: Padre Xifré, 5. Tel. 413 78 39.

Siddharta: Serrano, 45. Tel. 275 56 47.
Tartufo: Víctor Hugo, 5. Tel. 232 31 48.

Night Clubs

Windsor: Raimundo Fernández Villaverde, 65. Tel. 455 58 14.
Cleofás: Goya, 7. Tel. 27 45 23.
Pasapoga: Gran Vía, 37. Tel. 232 16 44.
La Trompeta: Gran Vía, 54. Tel. 247 11 30.
Caribiana: Paseo de la Castellana, 83. Tel. 455 77 69.
Xenon: Bajos Cine Callao. Tel. 231 97 94.
Molino Rojo: Tribulete, 16. Tel. 230 87 34.
Sambrasil: Avenida del Brasil, 5. Tel. 456 37 82.

Flamenco Clubs

Los Canasteros: Barbieri, 10. Tel. 231 81 63.
Corral de la Morería: Morería, 17. Tel. 265 84 46.
Corral de la Pacheca: Juan Ramón Jiménez, 26. Tel. 458 26 72.
Café de Chinitas: Torrija, 7. Tel. 248 51 35.
Torres Bermejas: Mesonero Romanos, 11. Tel. 232 33 22.
Venta del Gato. Carretera Madrid-Burgos, km. 7,7. Tel. 202 43 27.
Arco de Cuchilleros: Arco de Cuchilleros, 7. Tel. 266 58 67.

Comunication Media

ABC: Serrano, 61. Tel. 435 31 00.
Diario-16: San Romualdo, 26. Tel. 754 40 66.
El País: Miguel Yuste, 40. Tel. 754 38 00.
Ya: Mateo Inurria, 15. Tel. 259 28 00.
Televisión Española: Prado del Rey. Tel. 711 04 00.
Radio Nacional de España: Prado del Rey. Tel. 218 32 40.
S.E.R.: Gran Vía, 32. Tel. 232 28 00.
Radio Intercontinental: Modesto Lafuente. Tel. 254 46 03.
Radio España: Manuel Silvela, 9. Tel. 447 53 00.
Radio El País: Miguel Yuste, 40. Tel. 754 40 57.
Radio Minuto: Gran Vía, 31. Tel. 222 91 57.
COPE: Juan Bravo, 49, dpldo. Tel. 402 86 14.
Antena-3: Oquendo, 23. Tel. 411 70 11.
Radiocadena: Ayala, 17. Tel. 276 56 34.
Radio-80: Enrique Larreta, 5. Tel. 733 80 80.

Important Shops and department stores

G. A. El Corte Inglés: Preciados, 7. Tel. 232 18 00.

G. A. Galerías Preciados: Plaza Callao, 1.
Tel. 222 47 71.
G. A. Celso García: Serrano, 52. Tel. 275 42 05.
Cortefiel. Serrano 40. Tel. 431 33 42.
Loewe: Serrano, 26. Tel. 401 29 08.
Jesús del Pozo: Almirante, 28. Tel. 231 66 76.
Luis Gómez: O'Donell, 49. Tel. 274 28 41.
Don Carlos: Serrano, 92. Tel. 275 75 07.
Fancy Men: Serrano, 93. Tel. 262 18 67.
Givenchi: Concha Espina, 5. Tel. 250 24 78.
Gucci: Don Ramón de la Cruz, 2.
Tel. 431 17 17.
Lorca: Velázquez, 43. Tel. 431 99 42.
Robert Max: Milaneses, 3. Tel. 242 35 88.
Cacharel: Serrano, 88. Tel. 435 32 26.
Hermes: Ortega y Gasset, 26. Tel. 276 89 95.
Saint Laurent: Serrano, 100. Tel. 276 82 03.
Tres Zetas: Ortega y Gasset, 17. Tel. 431 11 43.
Artespaña: Gran Vía, 32.
Sargadelos: Zurbano, 46. Tel. 410 48 30.

Banks

España: Alcalá, 50. Tel. 446 90 55.
Central: Alcalá, 49.Tel. 232 88 10.
Bilbao: Paseo de la Castellana, 81.
Tel. 455 21 40.
Hispanoamericano: Plaza Canalejas, 1.
Tel. 222 46 60.
Español de Crédito: Paseo de la Castellana, 7.
Tel. 419 17 08.
Vizcaya: Alcalá, 45. Tel. 221 11 77.
Exterior de España: Carrera de San Jerónimo,
36. Tel. 429 44 77.
Popular: Alcalá, 26. Tel. 232 09 06.

Traditional Markets

The Rastro (Flea Market), selling all kinds of
objects. Plaza de Cascorro. Ribera de
Curtidores. On Sundays.
Craft Fair: Plaza de San Ildefonso. On Saturday
afternoons.
Cuesta de Moyano: Old and cheap books,
between Retiro Park and the Glorieta Carlos V.
Open every day.
Lithograph Fair. Plaza Mayor. Saturday
mornings.
Stamp Fair. Plaza Mayor. Sunday mornings.

Art Galleries

Abril: Arenal, 18. Tel. 221 14 37.
Aldaba; Rollo,7. Tel. 247 51 86.
Berkowitsch. Velázquez, 1.Tel. 275 64 31.
Biosca: Génova, 11. Tel. 419 33 93.

Cano: Paseo Prado, 26. Tel. 228 77 52.
Cacar: Almagro, 32. Tel. 410 45 77.
Celini: Bárbara de Braganza. Tel. 419 41 77.
El Coleccionista: Claudio Coello, 23.
Tel. 429 87 03.
Fauna's: Montalbán, 11. Tel. 222 60 02.
Fernando Vijandre: Núñez de Balboa, 65.
Tel. 435 80 25.
Fundación Juan March: Castelló, 77.
Tel. 435 42 40.
Juana Mordó: Villanueva, 7. Tel. 431 42 64.
Kreisler: Serrano, 19. Tel. 276 16 64.
Kreisler, 2. Hermosilla, 8. Tel. 431 42 64.
La Pinacoteca: Claudio Coello, 28.
Tel. 276 57 92.
Macarrón: Jovellanos, 2. Tel. 429 68 01.
Miguel Angel: Miguel Angel, 31.
Tel. 442 00 22.

Orfila: Orfila, 3. Tel. 419 88 64.
Rayuela: Claudio Coello, 19. Tel. 275 31 46.
Sargadelos: Zurbano, 46. Tel. 410 48 30.
Toisón: Arenal, 5. Tel. 232 16 16.
Tórculo: Claudio Coello, 17. Tel. 275 06 86.

Tourism Delegations and Agencies

Austria: Torre de Madrid, planta 11.
Tel. 247 89 24.
Belgium: Navas de Tolosa, 3. Tel. 221 26 81.
Bulgaria: Princesa, 12. Tel. 248 47 52.
Egypt: Alcalá, 21. Tel. 222 60 51.
England: Torre de Madrid,
planta 6.ª Tel. 241 13 96.
France: Alcalá, 63. Tel. 276 31 44.
Germany; San Agustín, 2. Tel. 429 35 51.
Holland: Apartado de Correos, 8101.
Tel. 241 28 85.
India: Torre de Madrid. Tel. 241 44 68.
Italy: Alcalá, 63. Tel. 276 80 08.
Mexico: Velázquez, 126. Tel. 261 18 27.
Panama: Edificio España. Tel. 248 96 49.
Poland: Torre de Madrid, Agencia Orbis.
Tel. 248 53 65.
Rumania: Alfonso XII, 157. Tel. 458 78 95.
South Africa. Tel. 247 65 79.
Switzerland: Edificio España,
planta 1.ªTel. 247 03 36.
Tunisia: Torre de Madrid. Tel. 248 18 43.

Aero Taxis

Aelyper, S. A.: Aeropuerto Cuatro Vientos, Ap.
27045. Tel. 208 99 40.
Helicópteros, S. A.: Aeropuerto Cuatro Vientos.
Tel. 208 81 40.
Jet-Alpa, S.A.; Aeropuerto de Barajas: Serrano,
41-2.ºTel. 255 76 05.
Navegación y Servicios Aéreos, S. A
Tel. 234 79 54.

Railway Stations

Renfe: Alcalá, 44. Information. Tel. 733 22 00.
Atocha: Glorieta Emperador Carlos V.
Tel. 733 30 00.
Chamartín: final de Agustín de Foxá.
Tel. 733 30 00.
Estación del Norte: Paseo de la Florida.
Tel. 247 00 00.
Nuevos Ministerios, enlaces: Paseo de la
Castellana. Tel. 233 78 92.

Chambers of commerce

Superior Board of Official Chambers of
Commerce: Claudio Coello, 19. Tel. 275 34 00.

Austria: Orense, 11. Tel. 233 58 07.
Belgium-Luxembourg: Rodríguez San Pedro, 13.
Tel. 446 81 35.
France: Serrano, 3. Tel. 225 93 20.
Germany: Barquillo, 17. Tel. 222 10 40.
Great Britain: Marqués de Valdeiglesias, 3.
Tel. 212 96 22.
Holland: Zurbarán, 10. Tel. 419 14 75.
Italy: Factor 1. Tel. 234 25 09.
Madrid: Plaza Independencia, 1. Tel. 232 10 11.
Mexico: San Agustín, 2. Tel. 232 50 78.
Netherlands: Zurbarán, 10. Tel. 419 14 75.
Poland: Serrano, 3. Tel. 431 90 93.
Sweden: Marqués de Casa Riera, 4.
Tel. 221 82 50.
Switzerland: Doctor Fleming, 55. Tel.
259 25 61.
United States: Padre Damián, 23. Tel.

158 65 59.
Venezuela: Paseo Habana, 17. Tel. 262 62 37.
Yugoslavia: Paseo Castellana, 177. Tel.
270 44 75.

Shipping Lines

Aucona: Alcalá, 63 y P. Muñoz Seca, 2.
Tel. 225 51 10.
Aznar: Alcalá, 61. Tel. 276 28 00.
Canguro Lines, Ybarra: Gran Vía, 8.
Tel. 222 91 70.
Cía. Gral. Trasatlántica: Viajes Conde. Gran Vía,
50. Tel. 247 18 04.
Cía. Nac. Argelina de Navegación: C. Bordiú,
19-21. Tel. 234 11 05.
Cía. Trasmediterránea: Zurbano, 73.

Tel. 254 66 00.
Cunard Line: Viajes Marsans. C. S. Jerónimo,
34. Tel. 231 18 00.
Italian Line: Viajes Awersari. Alcalá, 54.
Tel. 222 82 23.
Líneas Marítimas Alemanas: Viajes Norda. C. S.
Jerónimo, 27. Tel. 232 24 00.
Svenska Lloyd: Viajes Conde. Rafael Salgado, 3.
Tel. 250 29 42.
Swedish Lloyd: Alberto Jentoft. R. Salgado, 3.
Tel. 250 29 42.
Trasatlántica: Paseo Recoletos, 4.
Tel. 275 98 00.
Ybarra y Cía.: Bergé y Cía., Gran Vía, 8.
Tel. 222 91 70.

Foreign Railways

French Railways: Gran Vía, 57.
Tel. 247 20 20.
Swiss Federal Railways: Gran Vía, 88. Tel.
247 06 36.
West German Railways: Paseo de la Castellana,
1. Tel. 419 23 12.

Permanent tow truck service

Anda: Juan de Olías, 15. Tel. 216 54 27.
Autos Unidos: Ayala, 10. Tel. 225 67 91.
Cuadrado: Sambara, 136. Tel. 267 01 28.
De Juan: Zamora, 7. Tel. 459 20 32.
Europarke: Olite, 38. Tel. 233 74 74.
Nieto: Dolores Folgueras, 20. Tel. 203 41 39.
Pardal: Bocángel, 30. Tel. 246 76 05.
Sánchez: San Raimundo, 6. Tel. 459 72 28.
Zaragoza: Titania, 34. Tel. 200 19 38.

Pastry Shops

El Buen Retiro: Goya, 17. Tel. 435 72 82.
Caramelos Paco: Toledo, 55. Tel. 265 42 58.
La Casa de las Tartas: Alonso Heredia, 4.
Tel. 246 11 86.
Croissanterie: San Millán, 2. Tel. 265 08 49.
Formentor: General Díez Porlier, 7.
Tel. 431 97 27.
La Flor de Lys: Puerta del Sol, 11.
Tel. 222 54 02.
Habana: Cea Bermúdez, 57. Tel. 244 36 98.
Heladería Italiana Capri: Alb. Aguilera, 50.
Tel. 242 59 20.
Chocolates el Indio: Luna, 14. Tel. 221 41 99.
Jarabes Madrueño: Postigo S. Martín, 3.
Tel. 221 19 55.
Juncal: Recoletos, 15. Tel. 431 03 14.

Casa Mira, Turrones: Carrera San Jerónimo, 30.
Tel. 429 67 96.
Mónico: Gutiérrez Solana, 8. Tel. 261 78 88.
Neguri: Claudio Coello, 68. Tel. 275 58 75.
La Pajarita: Puerta del Sol, 6. Tel. 221 49 14.
Pastelería El Pozo: Pozo, 8. Tel. 222 38 94.
El Riojano: Mayor, 10. Tel. 266 44 82.
Rivas: Barquillo, 11. Tel. 221 04 69.
Samovar: Diego de León, 15. Tel. 251 73 70.
Bombonería Santa: Serrano, 56. Tel. 276 86 46.
La Violeta: Plaza Canalejas, 6. Tel. 222 55 22.

Shopping centers

Continente: Carretera de Burgos, km. 7.
Tel. 653 14 11.
Jumbo: Avda. Pío XII, 2. Tel. 259 03 00.
Macro: Crta. Barcelona, km. 11,30.
Tel. 747 47 11.
Madrid-2, «La Vaguada», Barrio del Pilar.
Tel. 730 50 33.

Take away food shops

Charlot: Claudio Coello, 87. Tel. 276 67 40.
L'Escargot: Capitán Haya, 20. Tel. 455 18 13.
Habana: Cea Bermúdez, 57. Tel. 449 30 87.
Mallorca: Bravo Murillo, 7. Tel. 448 97 49.
Velázquez, 59. Tel. 431 99 09.
Comandante Zorita, 39. Tel. 253 51 02.
Multicentro Orense, 6. Tel. 456 27 42.
Serrano, 88. Tel. 276 75 74.
Alberto Alcocer, 48. Tel. 458 75 11.
Rodilla: Princesa, 76. Tel. 244 32 27.
Viena: Marqués de Urquijo, 17. Tel. 248 51 90.
Viena Capellanes: Fuencarral, 122.
Tel. 446 17 83.